EVANSTON PUBLIC LIBRARY

3 1192 01199 7366

745.51 Odonn.L

O'Donnell, Liz.

Decorating turned wood :
the maker's eye /
c2002.

Decorating Turned Wood

The Maker's Eye

DATE DUE

MAR 3 1 2003	
JUN 1 3 2003	
JUN 2 6 2003	
FEB 1 1 2004	
JUN 1 6 2005	
FEB 0 6 2007	

DEMCO, INC. 38-2931

D1273719

FEB 1 2 2003

Decorating Turned Wood

The Maker's Eye

Liz & Michael O'Donnell

GUILD OF MASTER CRAFTSMAN PUBLICATIONS

EVANSTON PUBLIC LIBRARY
1703 ORRINGTON AVENUE
EVANSTON, ILLINOIS 60201

First published 2002 by
Guild of Master Craftsman Publications Ltd
Castle Place, 166 High Street,
Lewes, East Sussex BN7 1XU

Text © Liz and Michael O'Donnell 2002
© in the work GMC Publications 2002
Photographs by Joanne B. Kaar, Liz O'Donnell and
Michael O'Donnell, except pp. 18–19 and 34 by
Glyn Satterley, p. 146 by Malcolm Calder
Drawings and paintings by Liz O'Donnell
Diagrams by Michael O'Donnell

ISBN 1 86108 204 5

All rights reserved

The right of Liz and Michael O'Donnell to be identified as the
authors of this work has been asserted in accordance with the
Copyright Designs and Patents Act 1988, sections 77 and 78.

Whilst every effort has been made to obtain permission from
the copyright holders for all material used in this book, the
publishers will be pleased to hear from anyone who has not
been appropriately acknowledged, and to make the correction
in future reprints.

No part of this publication may be reproduced, stored in a
retrieval system or transmitted in any form or by any means
without the prior permission of the publisher and copyright
owner.

This book is sold subject to the condition that all designs are
copyright and are not for commercial reproduction without the
permission of the designer and copyright owner.

The publishers and author can accept no legal responsibility for
any consequences arising from the application of information,
advice or instructions given in this publication.

A catalogue record for this book is available from the
British Library.

Edited by Stephen Haynes
Book and cover designed by Fineline Studios
Set in Centaur and Stone Sans

Colour origination by Viscan Graphics (Singapore)
Printed and bound by Kyodo Printing (Singapore)

Contents

For Theresa
1911–2002

Warning

Although woodturning is safer than many other activities involving machinery, all machine work is inherently dangerous unless suitable precautions are taken.

Do not use timber which may come apart on the lathe – beware of faults such as dead knots, splits, shakes, loose bark, etc.

Avoid loose clothing or hair which may catch in machinery. Protect your eyes and lungs against dust and flying debris by wearing goggles, dust mask or respirator as necessary, but invest in an efficient dust extractor as well.

Pay attention to electrical safety; in particular, do not use wet sanding or other techniques involving water unless your lathe is designed so that water cannot come into contact with the electrics.

Keep tools sharp; blunt tools are dangerous because they require more pressure and may behave unpredictably.

It is not safe to use a chainsaw without the protective clothing which is specially designed for this purpose, and attendance on a recognized training course is strongly recommended.

Do not work when your concentration is impaired by drugs, alcohol or fatigue.

Dyes, stains and paints may contain harmful substances; protect yourself by wearing rubber gloves and working in well-ventilated surroundings at all times.

The safety advice in this book is intended for your guidance, but cannot cover every eventuality: the safe use of machinery and tools is the responsibility of the user. If you are unhappy with a particular technique or procedure, do not use it – there is always another way.

Measurements

Although care has been taken to ensure that the metric measurements are true and accurate, they are only conversions from imperial; they have been rounded up or down to the nearest whole millimetre, or to the nearest convenient equivalent in cases where the imperial measurements themselves are only approximate. When following the projects, use either the metric or the imperial measurements; do not mix units.

Introduction

Traditionally, wooden bowls were expected to be round, symmetrical and just as they come off the lathe, showing all the beauty of the natural wood. The idea that they could be cut, carved or decorated in some way was considered by many – in the UK, at least – to be a sacrilege, as it hides and destroys the colours and grain patterns of the wood. No doubt we ourselves fell into this category, always chasing after nicely figured wood for our turned bowls. However, in 1981, for health, environmental and economic reasons, we changed to working with mainly local trees. While these have their own distinctive character, dramatic they are not, and we could no longer rely on the startling grain patterns and colours of exotic wood to enhance the work. On the plus side, however, the plainer woods became our blank canvas, an ideal surface on which we could apply a variety of decorative treatments to create our own distinctive style of bowls and boxes.

This book documents our own journey along this route, from ideas, sketches, experimentation, trial and error, to the finished piece. By including pages from sketchbooks, working drawings and photographs of natural and man-made objects, we show what has influenced us and helped generate some of our ideas, giving an insight into some of the thought processes that are involved before we even touch a piece of wood. In doing this we hope to demonstrate that creativity is not something that some people have and others do not, but a skill that can be learned and developed like any other, and that design is simply a creative process which aims to turn an idea into something physical.

Every piece we make contains some elements of form, colour, pattern and texture, but for convenience we have grouped the work under these separate headings, where we feel that a piece of work best illustrates or emphasizes a particular element. We show the equipment and techniques we use for a variety of decorative processes, and illustrate the woodturning sequences involved in each project.

Chapter 1

Developing ideas

Inspiration can be a million ideas all hitting you at once, if you are lucky. It could be the result of a bit of lateral thinking: brainstorming, we find, helps free the mind of preconceptions or prejudice, the wild ideas being just as valuable as the sensible ones. It can be a mistake to dismiss ideas too early, because even the most bizarre may prove useful later on, and it is all worthwhile experience. New designs may also be the result of an obvious progression, whether it's a big leap or a small refinement based on past experience.

In order to develop these ideas we usually start by gathering information. This means taking photographs, making sketches, collecting postcards and cuttings from magazines, and gathering interesting found objects. In this way we have gradually built up a storage bank of visual images.

Photography

Subjects for photography could be anything with an interesting shape or a particular combination of colours and textures. These could be natural or man-made forms, such as seed heads, sand patterns, birds, buildings, machinery or boats. We also have a slide collection of other craftsmen's work as well as cuttings from magazines, but take the opportunity, when we can, to visit exhibitions, as seeing and handling the real thing is even more fascinating and rewarding. If a piece of work excites us, be it in glass, ceramics, metals, textiles or wood, we try to analyse why. Is it the shape, colour or texture?

We also use photography to document our own work – it's surprising how easily we forget what we have done in the past.

Rosehips in our garden in Caithness, Scotland

◀ **Exhibition of 200 Aboriginal burial poles, Sydney, Australia, 1988 – Australia's bicentennial year**

Detail of a fishing creel at Lybster harbour, Caithness

Tide flow,
Dunnet beach, Caithness

Close-up of a dry-stone wall at Fanore, Co. Clare, Ireland

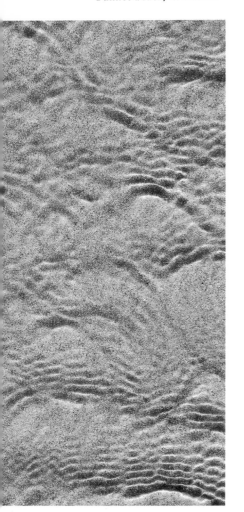

Photography is invaluable for recording shapes, colours and textures. Inspiration can be found in a wide range of natural and man-made forms

Historic skyline, Prague, Czech Republic

Boats tied up
in John o'Groat's
harbour, Caithness

Shop window,
Galway, Ireland

Detail of a winch mechanism at the Fossil Museum, Spittal, Caithness

Notebooks, sketches, found objects

Keeping a notebook, a bit like a visual diary – pasting or stapling photos, postcards and cuttings into a book, along with thumbnail sketches, working drawings or more detailed observational studies – creates a resource that we constantly add to and come back to periodically. When making these sketches we have to look closely, studying the shapes, colours and patterns. Drawing objects certainly improves visual awareness and helps develop our observational skills.

As inveterate beachcombers, we cannot resist taking home such treasures as shells, pebbles, skulls, driftwood – in fact, flotsam and jetsam of every description. They all add to our collection of visual stimuli.

Through teaching and running workshops we have had the chance to visit many countries that are as culturally, climatically and geographically diverse as Iceland and Australia. We have benefited both creatively and practically, because on returning home we have sometimes found that our work has taken on new directions and working methods.

This assorted collection of flotsam and jetsam is an example of the kind of observational study that can be an important source of new ideas – a storage bank, in other words. For instance, the intertwining fronds of seaweed emerge later, much simplified, as a sandblasted design on one of our jewellery boxes

These bird-related studies explore the different surface textures of each subject, such as the sharply pointed beak contrasting with the rounded, smooth dome shape of the bird's skull. The light airiness and delicate colouring of the feathers contrast with the roughness and tangled weaving of twigs and grasses, encircling and protecting the fragile eggs. This variety of textures – hard, soft, rough, smooth, light, chunky – is something we try to be aware of and introduce into our work. For instance, we vary the thickness of our bowls from paper-thin to rough and chunky, and experiment with different surface textures and finishes

Using the material

Making sketches and working drawings, we find, is a good starting point, especially when we are working together on a project. They give us a useful aid for discussion. They are also valuable if we are producing something for a friend or client, or collaborating with another craftsperson. Drawings are an instant means of communication: as they say,

'A picture speaks a thousand words.' When it comes down to designing a bowl, our thinking processes are not always logical, but can jump backwards and forwards in time. This is when we are able to refer to our notes, sketches and photographs. Sometimes we might retrieve an idea that we had tried before but not fully resolved.

◀ **A collection of carved, turned and decorated pieces – reminders of wonderful people and places we have visited**

A treasured possession: this David Pye bowl is a joy to hold. The grooves are hand-carved using his own invention, the 'fluting engine'

Our collection of oilcans, some originally used on British Rail

If a piece of work excites us, we try to analyse why. With Joanne Kaar's silk bowl it is the vibrant colours and the use of pyrography to create layers of overlapping spirals that we find interesting. The carved fish has painted stripes of flat colour with carved lines running parallel to these – a technique we tried later on some of our work. Metal oilcans are simple functional pieces which, surprisingly, were later to inspire a range of turned jewellery boxes

A souvenir of Australian Aboriginal art

A bowl in handmade silk paper by Joanne Kaar

Experimentation

The working drawings are just the beginnings; the next stage is the fun part: exploring in three dimensions, giving ourselves time to experiment with the materials, learning the practical skills necessary to use them, trying not to treat them too preciously but discovering their properties and making creative use of them. In most situations we are using conventional processes and materials we are familiar with, but combining them in new and innovative ways. Sometimes a new technique requires new equipment, but first we improvise with what we have around us in order to justify an investment at some later point.

The process of trial and error is an essential part of the development. Some of our ideas have evolved from what seemed to be just playing around with things, and even accidents can sometimes turn out to be beneficial. The more relaxed and adventurous we feel, the more chance there is of producing something exciting.

◀ **Studies of shells and sea urchins**

Sketchbooks with drawings of harbours and seabirds

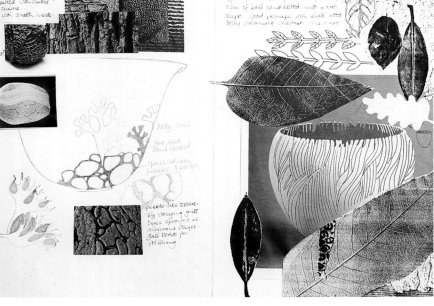

◀ **Developing ideas from leaf and pebble patterns**

A selection from our notebooks. By collecting together pictures, cuttings, sketches and more finished drawings we gradually build up a storage bank of visual images

▲ **Studies of pebbles, looking at colour and texture**

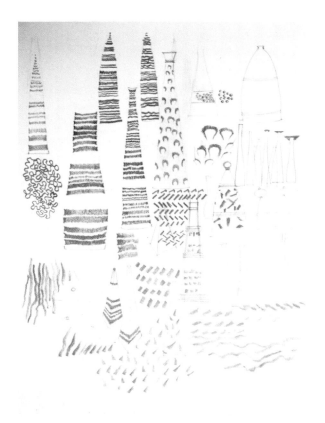

Drawings and sketches are a good place to start with a collaborative project: they stimulate discussion and help to convey ideas to the client in a way that mere words never can

◀ **Shapes and textures evolve quickly on paper, and the design can be refined before touching the wood**

With the working drawing complete, we are ready to start making the design in wood; it is all part of the development process

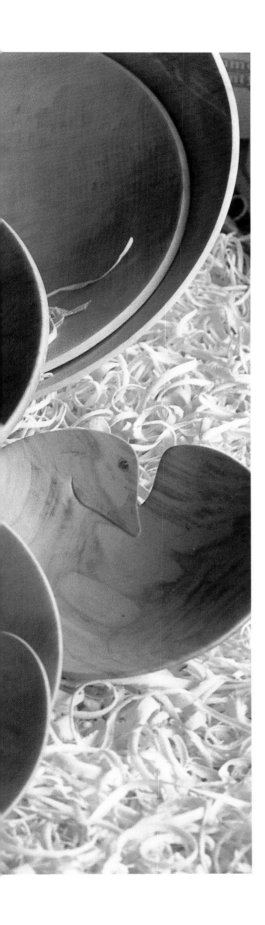

Chapter 2

Form

Wood is perhaps unique as a material, in that it seems to invite people to stroke and caress its surface. It's certainly true that to appreciate a form fully we do need to explore it through touch as well as sight, feeling its contours and experiencing the different textures with our fingertips.

When designing, we have to consider not only how a piece of work looks, but also what its purpose is. We are always striving to create forms that are both functional and visually stimulating, although we do believe that the function of a piece could simply be that it gives pleasure and raises one's spirits.

Ideas for forms may come from studying the infinite and subtle variations found in natural and man-made forms. Tall, elegant spires; squat, bulbous, narrow-necked seed heads; conical shells, and the softly rounded curves of toadstools and mushrooms, could all provide us with a wealth of inspiration. The shape of the tulips inspired the tulipwood bowl overleaf

Geometric series

Until 1980 we were producing functional turned pieces such as spinning wheels, spinning chairs, porridge spirtles and bowls – all items which you would expect to find in a Scottish croft, and made from West African kiln-dried wood. In January 1981 the well-known British turner Richard Raffan introduced us to turning green wood – that is, recently felled wood which has not been seasoned. We were greatly excited by this process, and keen to experiment with it ourselves, changing from using dry to green wood literally overnight.

One of our biggest and best purchases around this time was a tulipwood tree (*Liriodendron tulipifera*, magnolia family), which had been planted in a Victorian ornamental garden around 1860, only to be cut down 120 years later to make space for houses. This was in Dingwall, Ross and Cromarty, 100 miles south of where we live. The tree cost us £800 (in 1981), but it was 3ft (90cm) in diameter, weighed 6 tons (6000kg) and lasted us 18 months. We would cut off a slice every few days and carry it by wheelbarrow into the workshop, where it was cut into bowl blanks ready for turning.

This tulipwood was a wonderful wood to work, having deep purple, green and brown heartwood colours, which contrasted dramatically with the creamy sapwood.

When the tulipwood began to run out there were no obvious replacements around, and we were not keen to splash out large sums of money on decorative trees. Even if we could find them, living where we do, it would become an expensive and difficult logistical exercise. At this point, partly for environmental and economic reasons, we made a decision to use only local wood – mainly trees which had been cut down for housing, windblown or overgrown and untidy garden specimens. This was not such an obvious decision, as we live in Caithness, an almost treeless county in the far north of Scotland where the few sparse groups of trees – mainly sycamore, with some beech and ash – are particularly precious.

It was an exciting time and we were massively productive, turning more bowls than we had ever turned before, but working with green wood was not without its problems.

A tulipwood bowl made in 1981; the design exploits the contrast between the deep-coloured heartwood and the creamy sapwood. Height 6in (150mm)

Origin of the Geometric series

A pile of thin-walled holly bowls had accumulated. Holly is a beautiful wood, but it does have a tendency to split when your back is turned, and this was happening far too often. Solving the problem of how to avoid this in the first place was a priority, but what could we do with the numerous bowls we already had? We tried gluing them up, but the glue line was always visible. Making a feature of the split by using a coloured filler, such as an epoxy resin mixed with a powder colour, was another idea, but after trying this we weren't entirely happy with the results. The final option seemed to be throwing the bowls in the wood-burning stove, so at least we would get some heat out of them. But before their final demise, in desperation we doodled with a pencil, drawing shapes on the bowls; cutting the splits out altogether then seemed the obvious solution.

We drew lines in pencil around the splits, experimenting with different shapes, looking for dynamic and pleasing designs, particularly when viewed at eye level. After cutting out the shapes, the final results were far more attractive than the original bowls would have been; another dimension had been added and, hey presto, we had the beginnings of our Geometric series.

By this time we had solved the problem of the bowls splitting (mainly by changing the rim design: see below), and we even started cutting holes out of perfectly sound bowls. This gave us much more freedom to experiment and try out numerous variations. The cut-outs created a window to the inside of the bowl, making more interesting shadows and surfaces. Because it opened up the bowl, we then experimented with colour on the inside, creating a contrast and emphasizing the negative shape of the cut-out even more.

Colouring the rim with a permanent felt pen gave a nice crisp edge, drawing attention to the rim and encouraging the eye to follow the undulating line.

Rim shapes: the feathered edge is very prone to splitting during drying; the square edge is much more resistant to splitting

Redesigning a bowl whose rim has split while drying; the sketchbook helps us to explore the different possibilities

The cut-outs create interesting shadows and negative shapes, and the resulting interplay between inside and outside surfaces can be highlighted by the use of contrasting colours

Two beech bowls (1981/2) showing a simple geometric cut-out shape set off by a coloured interior. These don't rely on light shining on the inside, and can be viewed effectively from many different angles. The colouring was done with drawing inks, and the bowls are finished with Craftlac Melamine. Height 6in (150mm)

Sketchbook drawings exploring a variety of cut-out shapes on the rims

Technique

The bowl shapes we were working on initially were simple V-shapes, about 8in (200mm) in diameter, 3in (75mm) tall, and turned down to about ⅛in (3mm) thick. The turning procedure is shown on pages 58–9.

What we needed to do was to cut interesting shapes out of these thin wooden bowls. We had seen a similar process before in a jeweller's workshop, where they hand-cut delicate shapes from thin sheets of precious metals such as silver with a fine-bladed fretsaw. We made a support from a piece of 12 x 1in (300 x 25mm) wood, cut a V-shape in it and clamped this on a table. Using a coping saw we were then able to cut out simple shapes. As we were cutting very thin wood with a coarse coping saw, and the wood was supported from beneath, we fitted the blade so that it would cut on the pull stroke.

We also wanted to pierce narrow slits in the body of some of the bowls. As these did not come to the edge, we had to drill small holes at either end of the slot with an engineer's bit, then thread the coping saw blade through the hole, cutting as before.

The blades we used had a pitch almost the same as the wood thickness; this was not ideal, but it did the job for a while and got us started. They left a fairly rough finish, so we smoothed and refined the shapes with abrasive wrapped around a holder, either flat or round; we used this like a file, starting with 100-grit abrasive and working down to 240-grit.

This technique is very simple and can be done perfectly adequately using only small hand tools.

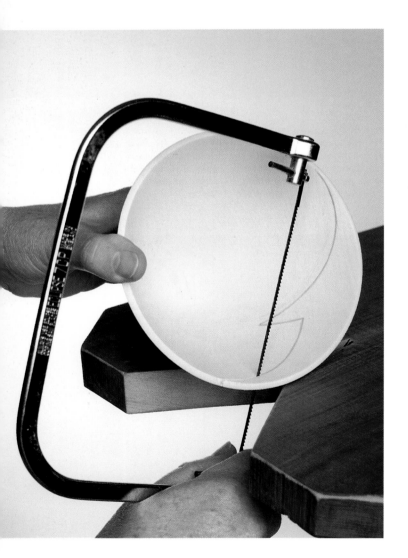

Cutting out the rim shape with a coping saw. A wide board of Parana pine, with a V-shaped notch to clear the saw blade, provides support. Note how the saw teeth point towards the handle

Sycamore bowls (2001) with acrylic stain on the inside
and rims emphasized in felt-tipped pen. The combination
of geometric cut-outs with the striking colour contrast
does give a dramatic effect. Height 5in (125mm)

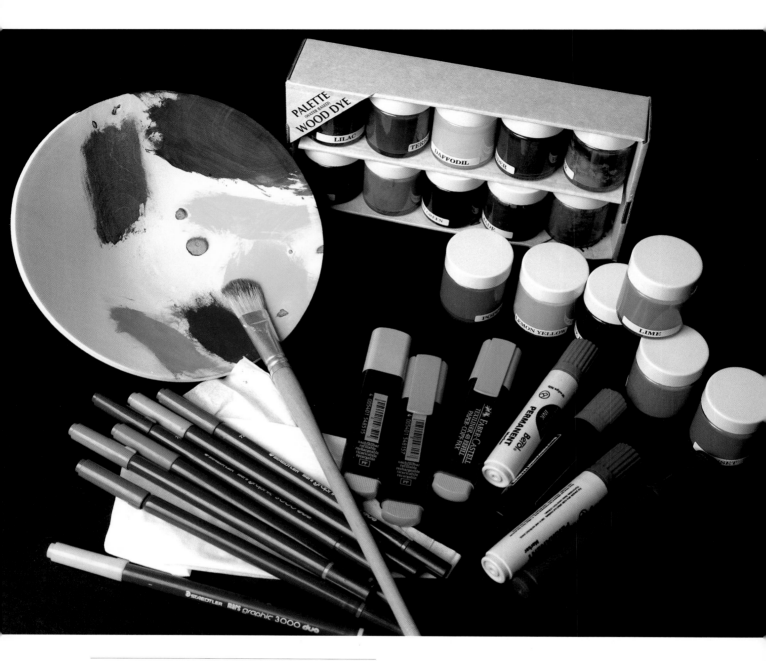

Testing the stains on a reject bowl first helps reduce disasters; these stains are water-based acrylic

Staining

We use an acrylic wood stain for colouring these bowls, mixing enough to complete the job and diluting it with a little water first. We like to have the wood grain showing through a nice, even, slightly transparent colour. As some of the colours seem more opaque than others, mixing them can involve a bit of trial and error; testing the stains on a reject bowl first helps reduce disasters.

Dab the cloth into the stain and wipe it on quickly and evenly. If the colour looks too pale when it dries, a second coat will deepen the colour. The acrylic stain dries very quickly, so in less than an hour the rim can be sanded, taking off any surplus stain to leave a nice clean edge ready for the felt-pen line. We prefer to use zingy, contrasting colours for this, for maximum impact.

Dab the cloth into the stain and wipe it on quickly and evenly. If the colour looks too pale when it dries, a second coat will deepen the colour. Always remember to wear protective rubber gloves when working with dyes and stains

Using felt-tipped pens to colour the rim. We prefer to use vibrant contrasting colours for this: it's definitely the 'wow' factor we want here

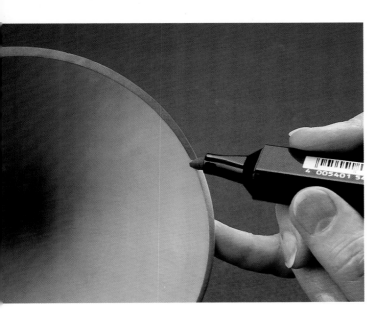

Materials

Acrylic wood stain

Felt-tip pens

Equipment

Coping saw or fretsaw with fine-toothed blade

Cutting board, home-made

Abrasives, 100 to 240 grit

Engineer's drill bit, $\frac{5}{32}$in (4mm)

Soft cloth or kitchen roll to apply the stain

Saucers or small dishes for mixing

Rubber gloves

Bird series

Quite where the idea came from we can't pin down, but it must have been a combination of living on a croft – keeping our own geese, ducks and hens, observing the wild birds around us, particularly the gannets diving around the boat when we are out fishing – and the 'pull-a-bird' toy we saw at a craft market in Covent Garden, London. Wherever it came from, we realized that our Geometric series of bowls could be developed into bird forms, and it was a small step from drawing geometric shapes to drawing simple stylized bird forms.

We used the grain patterns, which varied considerably from bowl to bowl, to decide where the bird's head and other features would be. Since the grain patterns on the finished bowls depend on how they were cut from the tree, we were soon able to cut the blanks to give us the grain patterns we wanted. (For detailed information on this, see Michael O'Donnell, *Turning Green Wood* (Lewes: GMC Publications, 2000), pages 12–15.) Sometimes a small defect in the wood might become an eye or a beak.

Two doves, with their eyes indicated by drilling. These are turned cross-grain in spalted beech and finished in Craftlac Melamine, without painting. Diameters 6in (150mm) and 4in (100mm), both 6in high and ⅛in (3mm) thick. 1984–5

A group of our own ducks

Much of the inspiration for our Bird bowls came from observing the ducks and geese on our own smallholding

Bird bowls in various stages of completion. The simplest
bowls were the small ducks, which had quite a large piece
cut out of the side. The base was angled to compensate,
and this brought the birds to life. These bowls in cross-
grain sycamore were made in 1984–5. Oil paint is used for
the details, and they are finished in Craftlac Melamine

From abstract geometric forms we soon progressed to drawing stylized bird shapes; our first bowls of this kind were made in January 1984

Developing ideas for the Bird bowls: simplifying the heads and wings

Other Bird bowls became very elaborate, with extensive shaping. As these were only about ⅛in (3mm) thick, they were too thin to carve. This one, made in 1984, was turned green from local sycamore, used cross-grain, and finished with oil paint and Craftlac Melamine. The diameter is 12in (305mm)

Dove in heavily spalted beech, turned cross-grain. 10in (255mm) diameter by 4½in (115mm) high. Craftlac Melamine with a very small amount of oil paint on beak and eye

The beautiful markings of spalted beech almost eliminate the need for painting; these designs rely on the cut-out shapes and a little carving, sometimes with drilled holes to emphasize the eyes

The first birds were small and simple in shape but had a lot of detail painting on the head and wing feathers. From this we developed a more minimal style by reducing the painting to the eyes and beaks only, relying more on the cut shape to suggest, rather than define, the bird form, and leaving more to the imagination. The simplest bowls were the small ducks, which had quite a large piece cut out on one side. By adjusting the alignment of the base in order to raise the cut-out side of the bowl, the balance of the bowl was restored, making a very dynamic piece. Small modifications like this can

sometimes make an enormous difference to the finished piece.

With the beautifully marked spalted woods, we eliminated painting altogether, relying only on the cut-out shapes and a little carving, and sometimes drilling holes to emphasize the eyes.

On the early thin bowls, the carving we could do was limited to very shallow V-grooves which we used to extend the feather shapes and give a little low relief to part of the head. Making the bowls thicker – up to ¼in (6mm) – allowed us to incorporate more carving, adding another

When out fishing, we had watched in awe as the gannets dived vertically into the water around our boat. We could never manage to get a really close look, only what we could see through the binoculars. Imagine how fortunate we felt to discover the body of this superb diver on the beach. We now had the opportunity to make detailed pastel and pencil studies, marvelling at the strong, bluish-grey beak, the startling blue legs and feet and the soft buff-yellow head. All these characteristics were emphasized and outlined with a 'designerish' black line

dimension to the work, and simultaneously making the bowls more robust and practical.

One of our favourite pieces is based on a gannet. We arrived at this particular design after turning a large bowl, 20in (500mm) diameter by 5in (125mm) high, only to discover an area of rotten wood. This was a special piece, earmarked for an exhibition at the Arrowmont 1985 seminar in America, so, with time running out, and not having any more wood of that size, we set about designing the bird so that the rotten bit would be cut out. There is nothing like desperation to get the creative juices flowing!

Pencil study of the gannet. The photograph allowed us to make very detailed studies of the head and the powerful beak (previous page)

Our first gannet bowl, made for the woodturning seminar at the Arrowmont School of Arts and Crafts, Gatlingburg, Tennessee, 1985. Sycamore, 19½in (495mm) diameter, painted in oils and finished with three sprayed coats of Craftlac Melamine

The gannet is such a large, dynamic bird that we felt the bowl would need to be fairly large in diameter and thick enough for some detailed carving on the head and feathers

Technique

When we begin to try out a new idea, there is always another tool or piece of equipment needed for the job – inevitably something we haven't got – but, as we like to strike while the iron is hot, we look around the workshop and house for tools that will get us through that experimental stage. We don't go out and buy special equipment for the job at that point – not that we could do, as our nearest big do-it-yourself supplier is over 100 miles away. It is surprising how much you can improvise while you decide whether an investment in equipment would be worthwhile. So a big distance from suppliers is not always a bad thing.

Now, with the Bird series requiring a lot more cutting out, it was time to invest in an electrically driven scrollsaw; this was a dream to use, and speeded up our production rate. It was great for the shallow bowls, but we still had to use the handsaw for the tall, narrow bowls, where access was impossible with the scrollsaw.

All our early carving was done with a surgical scalpel, using various blade shapes; this was cheap and effective on the thin bowls. As we increased the thickness of the bowls we added the use of hand scrapers to thin down larger areas and give a three-dimensional effect to the bird's head and feathers.

Our hand scrapers are ⅛in (3mm) thick hardened silver steel, and started about 8in (200mm) long. The narrow ones, adapted from planer blades, are ½in (13mm) wide, and the wider ones 2in (50mm). All the cutting edges are curved, depending on the application, and sharpened on a high-speed grinder to give a 45° bevel angle with a burred edge.

Though we got the results we wanted from these carving methods, we felt it was an appropriate time to look at power carving. We use two methods. The first is the power carver, which is a chisel blade

Our new Hegner scrollsaw makes cutting out the shape much easier than with the hand coping saw. It is easier to follow the fine pencil lines, and the scrollsaw leaves a finer finish. The foot control leaves both hands free to manœuvre the bowl, which is particularly important when the bowls are thin

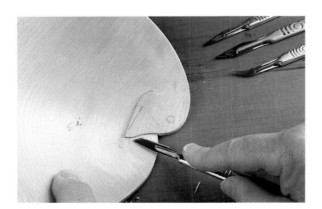

Scalpels were our main carving tools at first, because we already had them in the workshop and they were fine enough to work on the delicate bowls. We had to take light cuts and support the bowl carefully, as the thin bowls were very flexible and could all too easily be broken

More recently, we have started using a Proxxon power chisel, which makes the surface carving much quicker and less strenuous

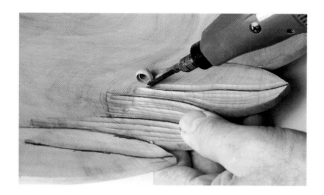

mounted in a power-operated hammer which produces up to 200 strokes per minute, making it possible to take long cuts in one easy action. We use this for bulk removal on the thicker bowls. For the finer work and on thinner bowls we use an ultra-high-speed rotary burr. We still use the hand scrapers for final shaping.

On the small birds, the realignment of the base, mentioned above, was done on the pillar drill. The table was tilted, the head slackened so that it was free to swing, and a 6in (150mm) diameter sanding disk was held in the Jacobs chuck. Holding the bowl upside down on the table by hand with the machine switched on, the sanding disc was lowered and swung over the base until it had flattened the whole surface to the new base angle. All the bases were then slightly dished with the hand scrapers so that the bowl would be stable.

The hand scrapers we used were the same ones we had used for the turning. The sharp edge refined the shape and left a smooth finish, ready for a final sanding down to 240-grit paper

A power sanding disc mounted in the lathe headstock made quick work of refining and smoothing the outside shape. For this very dusty operation it is essential to wear a mask and have the dust extractor running

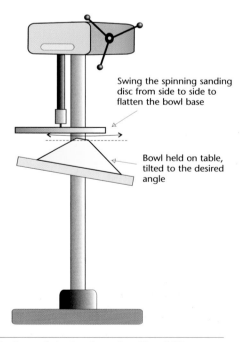

Swing the spinning sanding disc from side to side to flatten the bowl base

Bowl held on table, tilted to the desired angle

Realigning the base of the bowl on the pillar drill

We are constantly debating what kind of finish to use, but spraying on 3–5 coats of Craftlac Melamine is our usual procedure for the Bird bowls. Lacking a spray booth, we work outside. A light rub with worn 240-grit abrasive between coats, then finish with a fine wire wool after the last coat

Working from Liz's colour drawings, a fine sable brush and oil paint puts the final touches to the gannet's head, eye and beak

After carving, we sand the surfaces down to 240-grit abrasive to remove all tool marks and make a uniform surface for applying a final finish. As these are decorative pieces, we prefer a hard finish which gives durability and ease of cleaning. For this we spray on three fine coats of Craftlac Melamine, a cellulose-based lacquer containing particles of melamine, which gives a tough surface. We give a light rub down with a worn 240-grit abrasive between coats, usually allowing an hour for each coat to dry. Though the melamine dries in about 15 minutes, it takes about 5 days for it to harden fully, so we leave them for a week before lightly smoothing and matting the final coat with 400-grade wire wool to give the surface finish. We don't use wire wool between coats, as it breaks up in use, and sometimes small pieces remain on the surface and become trapped when the next coat is applied. This is a problem we don't have with a regular abrasive.

The painting of the beak and eye is done with oil paints and a fine sable brush, blotting off excess paint with a folded tissue. We use oil paint here because it gives a nice soft sheen, and when thinned with linseed oil it has a transparent quality, ideal for the bird's head. This is painted on top of the melamine spray finish, as spraying on top of the oil paint would lift it off. The oil paint will take a few days to harden properly.

Blotting the surface with a tissue removes excess paint and leaves a slightly transparent finish

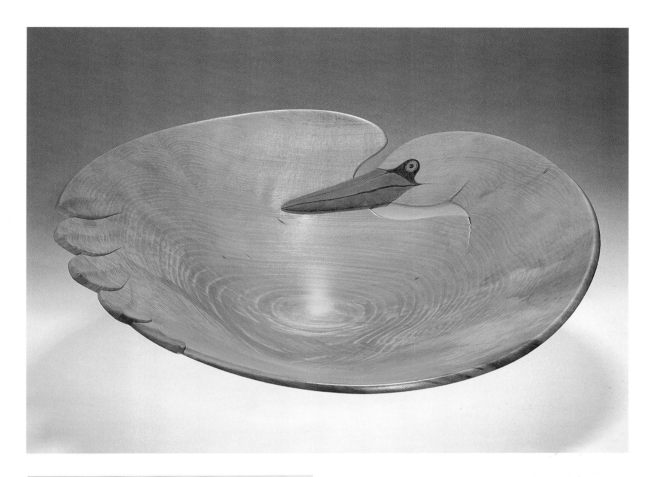

The elegant final result is a powerful representation of the gannet we found on the beach. Cross-grain sycamore, diameter 19½in (495mm), painted in oils and sprayed with three coats of Craftlac Melamine. 2001

Materials

Oil paint

Paper tissue

Turpentine

Linseed oil

Craftlac Melamine

Equipment

Good-quality sable brushes, sizes 1 and 4

Plate for mixing oil paint

Surgical scalpels with a selection of blade shapes

Hand scrapers with various edge shapes

Proxxon reciprocating chisel MSG 220 with V-cutter

Hegner scrollsaw

Pillar drill with tilting table

6in (150mm) sanding disc to fit in a Jacobs chuck

Proxxon rotary carver FSB 230/E with ⁵⁄₁₆in (8mm) burr

Shell series

Living close to the sea as we do, beachcombing has given our family hours of pleasure. Collecting shells, driftwood, pebbles, and searching for the elusive cowrie, locally named the *groatie buckie*, is always fun. Shells, found in such a wide variety of shapes and patterns from soft, sun-washed pastel colours to bold, jazzy spirals, are an endless, ever-changing source of delight and inspiration.

The top-shell is one we are always picking up and bringing home. This has a conical shape with a spiral band running around it which, when you look closely, resembles the pattern of a twisted rope or an Eastern turban.

A spiral form with overlapping surfaces, incorporating the use of coloured stripes, was the beginning of a design for our next group of bowls.

◀ **Shells provide a wealth of inspiration because they offer such a wide variety of shapes and patterns. The sea urchins we gathered while diving along the Caithness coast**

The spiral form of the top-shell recalls a rope or a turban

◀ **We are inveterate collectors, particularly when walking along the local beaches. Shells of all kinds, sea potatoes, even sea-worn shells which have eroded into interesting forms – we can't keep them all, but the photographs are a constant reminder**

A few sketches brought ideas together, all reflecting the top-shell theme. The initial drawings were based on a simple V-shape, echoing the conical outline. We tried various spiral rim shapes, flowing them over the inside surface of the bowl, finally adding a stripy band to emphasize the spiral. This was painted on the rim and along the carved overlapping edge. As most of the cut-out would be on one side of the bowl, tilting it slightly to raise the lower edge would give the bowl a better balance – a technique we had already tried on previous pieces and found successful.

Another shell with a more elongated shape led us to try a similar design on taller vessels, but this time with the spiral overlapping the outer surface.

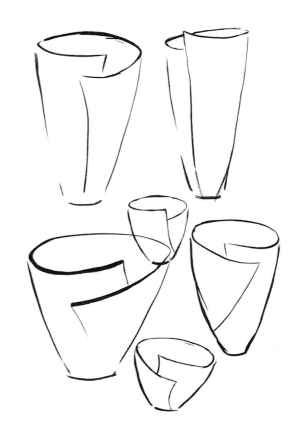

Quick sketches looking at overlapping shapes

Developing ideas for the Shell series: here we are looking at both the form and the possibilities for decoration

◀ For the first of the Shell series we used spalted sycamore, which recalls the natural environment amongst the seaweed on the shore

Three Shell bowls, each tilted slightly differently; this gives them all different characters, but they are still obviously from the same family. Turned cross-grain in spalted sycamore, finished with acrylics and Danish oil. 1987

Two more of the Shell series, with a slight variation on the carved form. Cross-grain sycamore, acrylics and Danish oil. 1987–8

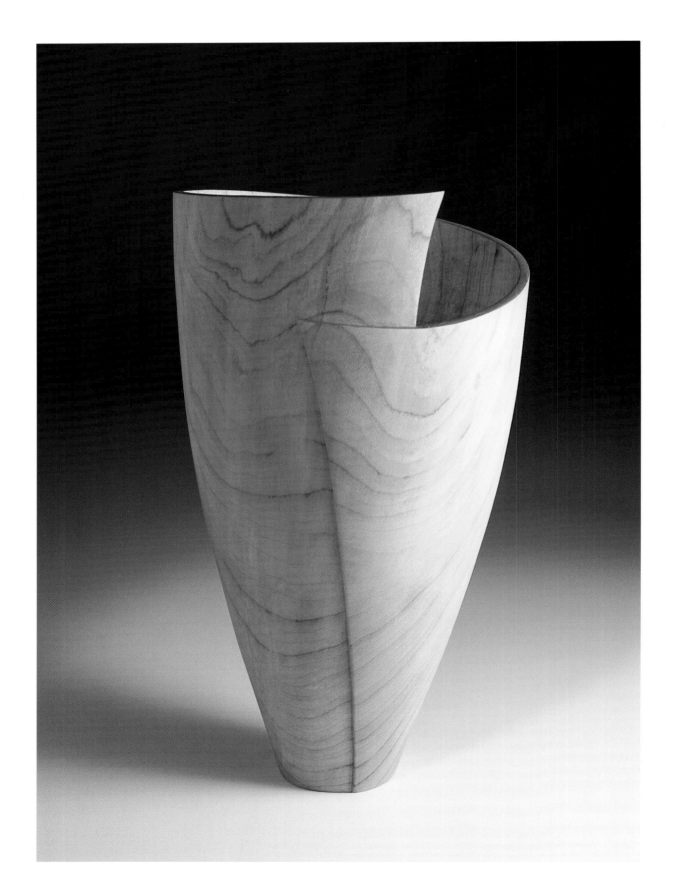

◄ A tall vessel in the same style, but with the carved spiral to the outside, makes an elegant piece. End-grain sycamore, acrylic paint and Danish oil. 1998

A Shell series bowl in cross-grain sycamore, finished with acrylic paint and Danish oil. 2001

Technique

In these bowls the colouring is applied to the rim surface only. To have any impact, the rim needs to be over ¼in (6mm) wide. This thickness also allows carving to create the spiral effect.

The carving technique is exactly the same as used on the Bird bowls: power tools, scalpels and hand scrapers, finishing with a 240-grit abrasive.

After carving, we decorate the rim using acrylics. We prefer acrylic paint here for several reasons:

- It sits on the surface of the wood and does not bleed.
- It dries quickly.
- We like the matt finish.
- The range of colours is limitless.
- It is hard-wearing and will withstand knocks.
- The colours have a chalkiness which seems appropriate for shells.

For these bowls we went for a softer matt oil finish (liquid paraffin) which could be applied after the painting.

The basic technique for the tall bowls is the same as for the birds, except that the detail is carved with the Proxxon power chisel before cutting the rim to shape. This allows the piece to be held firmly in a vice, which makes the job both easier and quicker

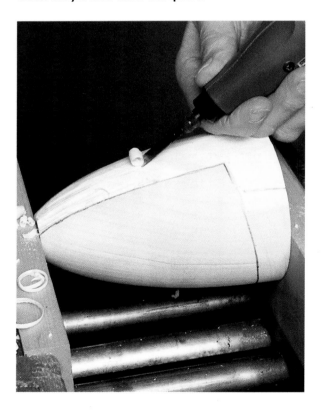

Developing ideas further: using pattern to highlight the rim

Painting the rim defines the form; a wide rim makes space for the pattern and allows for greater depth of carving. A fine brush is used to apply the acrylic paint

Materials

Acrylic paint in tubes

Danish oil or liquid paraffin

Equipment

Hegner scrollsaw

Scalpels

Hand scrapers

Proxxon reciprocating chisel MSG 220 with
    V-cutter (optional)

Pillar drill

Good-quality fine sable brushes, sizes 1 and 3

Mixing plate

Turning sequence for cross-grained bowls

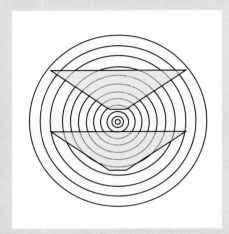

1   Position of the bowls in the log

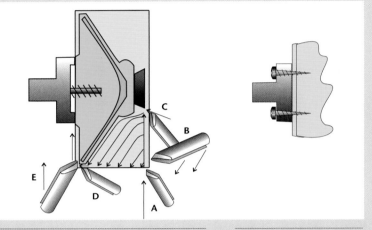

2   First mounting on a single-screw chuck

A   Clean across the bottom surface

B   Rough out the outside bowl shape

C   Cut the spigot for the second chucking

D   True up the edge of the blank

E   Trim up the top surface down to the chuck

2a Alternative first mounting on faceplate or multi-screw chuck

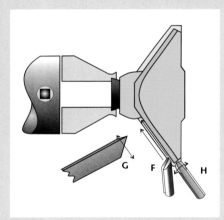

3   Second mounting on spigot in four-jaw chuck (O'Donnell jaws)

F   Final trim down the outside to be sure it is running true

G   Sheer-scrape up and down the outside with a skew scraper to give a fine finish

H   Roll the gouge on the rim, with bevel contact underneath the cutting edge

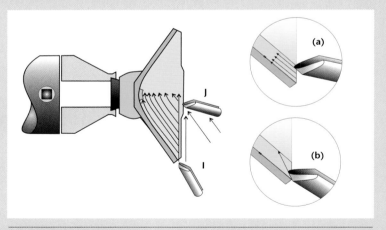

4   Turning the inside

I   Trim across top surface

J   Turn the inside with a series of cuts following the outside shape

4a and b Alternative methods of starting the last cut on the inside when the bowl is very thin

(a) Make a few short cuts of gradually increasing depth, then take the whole cut in one go

(b) Chamfer the edge so that the last cut will start fine then build up to the full thickness

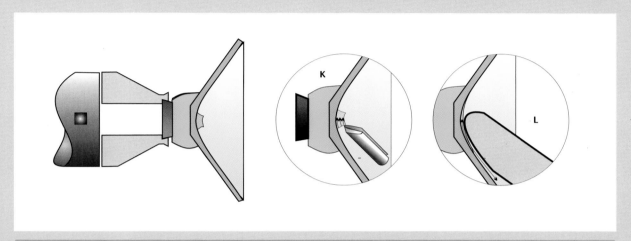

5 Finishing the inside

K Remove the last bit in the bottom with the gouge

L Final smoothing and shaping with the curved scraper

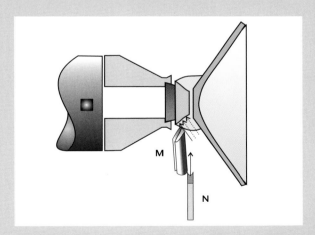

6 Finishing the base and parting off

M Remove the last bit of wood from around the base

N Part off

This completes the tool sequence for making the bowl. In addition, sanding is needed at each stage when the surface is finished.

Chapter 3

Colour

We are surrounded daily by a feast of colour, from the muted, soft, sea-washed pinks and greys in a pebble to the dramatic, hot reds and oranges of a glorious sunset. Beautiful colour combinations can be seen, not only in fine art but in simple everyday objects, which can unexpectedly surprise and inspire us.

A useful division of colours is into warm colours – those tending towards yellow or red – and cool colours; those inclining to or containing blue. If we want to create a harmonious and subtle effect, then combining a number of colours from only one of these groups will do the trick.

Complementary colours, such as blue and orange, are opposite each other on the colour circle, and these show each other off dramatically. When they are placed next to each other they can really shout. We use these if we are aiming for a bold contrast, for instance on the inner and outer surfaces of a bowl.

Colours can be divided into two main groups: warm colours, containing yellow or red, and cold colours, inclining to blue

We can find interesting colour combinations in unexpected places

The spectacular colours of a Caithness sunset

Subtle combinations in the natural colours of seaweed

A watercolour study of two cabbages. Simple, everyday things may sometimes inspire us. We love the colour combinations in these two cabbages: one cool greens and yellows, the other warm purples and pinks

The exciting colour combinations of this Irish house suggested colours for one of our Geometric series

Pebbles on the beach at John o'Groat's, Caithness, Scotland. The mottled pinks and greys could be translated into one of our Marbled series

◄ This embroidered Indian textile panel with its warm golden tones has inspired us to use a similar range of colours on some of our Coloured series of thin-walled vessels, such as the one shown below

Coloured series bowl in end-grain sycamore, pith not included. Brusho water-based batik fabric dyes and Craftlac Melamine

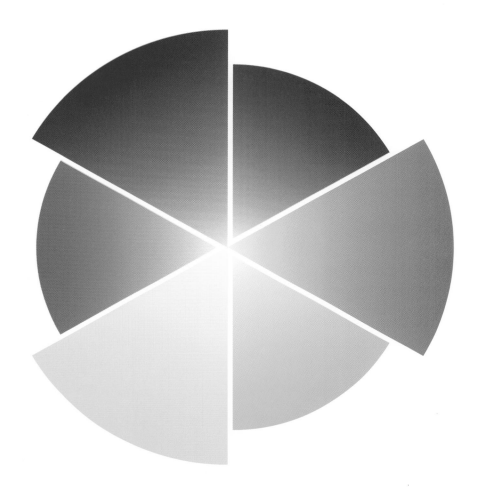

Two versions of the colour circle, showing the three primary colours red, yellow and blue, and the secondary colours formed by mixing them. Colours which fall opposite each other on the colour circle, such as blue and orange, are said to be complementary, and can be used to advantage when a strong contrast is required

Coloured series

By this time we had turned so much sycamore and holly that the whiteness was losing its appeal. We began experimenting with colour and trying different methods of application. This was great fun, splashing on colour while the bowl spins in the lathe (wear protective clothing), or saturating the inside of the bowl with ink, then switching on the lathe.

As it spins it forces the colour through the grain of the wood to the outside. Both surfaces were then turned, leaving the colour embedded in the grain. We used multiple colours, dabbing them on with cloths and sponges to give the colour some texture, creating some wonderful accidental effects. Playing with paint isn't just for four-year-olds at nursery!

◄ **If we are looking for harmonious and subtle colour combinations, then colours which are grouped close together on the colour wheel are appropriate. Coloured series bowl in end-grain sycamore, with pith in the centre, finished with Brusho water-based batik fabric dyes and Craftlac Melamine**

A dramatic contrast of complementary colours on a Coloured series bowl. Turned end-grain in sycamore, pith not included; Brusho water-based batik fabric dyes and Craftlac Melamine

Some of our early experiments in colouring techniques

When we first experimented with colour in 1982 we tried food colouring, inks and then fabric dyes – all items we could find lying around at home – and this got us started quickly. These were easy to use, and they could either be diluted down to a pale wash, or used concentrated to create strong, intense colours which still allowed the grain to show through. Today, twenty years on, there is a bewilderingly wide range of wood colour dyes, stains and varnishes available. As we were colouring cross-grained bowls at this time – that is, with the grain running across the bowl from side to side – we discovered that there was much better colour penetration on the end-grain sections than on the

Spattered bowl: ink was splashed on while the piece was rotating in the lathe

An early piece stained inside with green ink; interesting turned detail highlights the rim

Two contrasting colours of ink can be dabbed on with a cloth or sponge

This bowl was saturated with colours before switching on the lathe

cross-grain parts, which made them look patchy and uneven. Disappointed with this, we left the problem unresolved on the back burner until 1989, when we were in Norway for the first Scandinavian Woodturning Seminar.

Here we were exposed to a totally different woodturning tradition. The Norwegians used hook tools which were quite different from our woodturning tools; however, the main difference that caught our imagination was that the bowls were turned end-grain – that is, with the grain running vertically through the bowl. Not only that, but there was a long tradition in the use of colourful decoration on bowls, platters and drinking vessels.

Norway has a long tradition of painted decoration on bowls, platters and drinking vessels. This group of modern pieces dates from around 1987–8; the bowl at top right was turned by Hans Lee from Oslo

A traditional Norwegian vessel from the collection of Hans Lee

End-grain turned bowl with a hollow foot; traditional Russian decoration, c.1890

They used an oil-based paint which gives a soft sheen finish, and the designs were often stylized plant forms executed with loose brush strokes, reminiscent of barge painting in Britain.

As soon as we arrived home we tried turning an end-grain bowl and colouring it to see if we got acceptable results. Unfortunately we turned the rim of the first bowl too thin and it began splitting in a few places, following down the grain. As this was purely an experimental piece, we looked for a method of stopping the splits running progressing further. Drilling a hole at the end of the split would do the job, but it was a delicate bowl and drilling would be difficult. Earlier that day we had been using a pyrography machine to sign pieces, so we hit on the idea of burning a hole at the end of each split. This worked perfectly: not only did it stop the splits, but it left an interesting black surface texture which we could then use to create irregular rims. This black edge seemed to work like the lead in stained glass, separating and enhancing the colours.

The charred black rims bring out the glowing colours rather like the lead in a stained-glass window. The burnt edge was originally an attempt to save the first experimental bowl which had some splits in it

Bottoms up! We made our first end-grain bowl with a round bottom to reduce the risk of stress and splitting around the pith – the same reason that the foot of the Russian bowl was hollowed

The first experimental bowl, which we still have, was made deliberately with a rounded bottom in order to reduce the internal stresses and splitting which can occur while the bowl is drying. This is more likely to happen when the pith of the tree is present in the middle of the bowl (see *Turning Green Wood*, pages 8–11). Since we liked the movement it created, we continued with the round bottom feature for the rest of the series.

Some of the Scandinavian bowls we saw were footed, and the feet were hollowed for the same reason, to reduce stresses and therefore prevent splitting. We also made some footed bowls, carving away part of the foot to create legs.

Four-legged bowl, Coloured series. Turned end-grain in sycamore, pith not included. Brusho water-based batik fabric dyes and Craftlac Melamine

A group of Coloured series bowls in end-grain sycamore, pith not included. Brusho water-based batik fabric dyes and Craftlac Melamine

The colouring was a great success, which we continued to develop using a product called Brusho. This is a very concentrated powder intended for batik and tie-dye. We tend to prefer these water-based colours: we find them easy to use, and they lend themselves to mixing and blending. They are also suitable for using on wet wood, and are compatible with the sprayed cellulose finish which we often use. But it all comes down to personal preference, no doubt.

By dabbing on household bleach with a crumpled tissue, an old brush or even wooden toothpicks, we created even more fascinating colour changes and patterns.

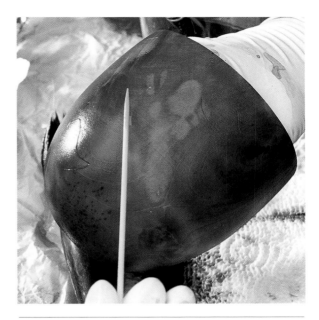

Dabbing on bleach with a stick to modify the colour

This series of functional bowls with just a coloured rim was probably a reaction to the fully coloured and decorative (non-functional) Coloured series bowls. Turned end-grain in sycamore, pith not included. Finished with acrylic paint and vegetable oil. 1992

Technique

The technique for turning the end-grain bowls is slightly different from that for turning cross-grain. The wood is first held between centres to rough out the shape and prepare for the second chucking, which could be either a faceplate or a four-jaw chuck. The third chucking, to finish the bottom, is on the rim, using wooden jaws attached to the four-jaw chuck, or a jam-fit chuck. The stages are illustrated on pages 96–7.

There are two options for cutting end-grain bowls from the tree. The easiest is to make a bowl only a little smaller than the diameter of the log. This would place the pith of the tree in the bottom of the bowl, and it could be exactly in the centre if you place the drive centres there. The other option is to mark out much smaller blanks away from the pith.

Colouring

The colouring process is very fast, so it is important to have all the necessary equipment to hand at the start: paint, rubber gloves, apron, sponges, brushes, rags, water.

It's best to wet the bowl first, using a sponge or a large brush, before applying the colour; this helps the colour spread without leaving any hard edges. Take a large brush which holds plenty of colour and slosh it on quickly, covering, say, 75% of the bowl surface in patches.

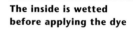

The inside is wetted before applying the dye

Colouring equipment: Chinese and Western brushes, water-based dyes, sponge, palette knives, pyrography unit

Applying the first colour to the inside ▶

If you are using two colours, then this is the time to drop in the next one, tipping the bowl in different directions as the colours mix and run together, creating accidental combinations. If it is too runny and difficult to control, dab it with a sponge to soak up the excess liquid. Applying colour to thin-walled, wet bowls means that the dye penetrates the wood, resulting in interesting spots and speckles on the opposite side. This can be used to great effect by simply applying a single colour to the inside, then allowing it to dry slightly before applying another colour to the outer surface.

We are often asked about the problem of raising the grain when wetting wood, but for us this has never been a problem, probably because we are turning the wood 'green' in one operation. If we were to use kiln-dried wood for turning, then perhaps it could be a problem.

Wetting the outside; note spots of colour penetrating from inside

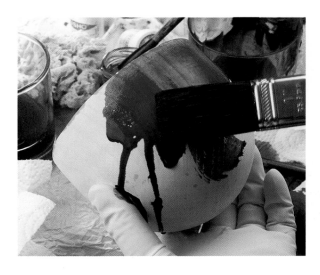

Brushing the first colour on the outside

Adding a contrasting colour to the outside

Burning

Our pyrography machine has an electrically heated wire tip which can be finely controlled so that it can be used for drawing and writing on wood. If the heat is turned up to the maximum, the tip glows almost white and can then be used for cutting and carving thin bowls. To pierce the wood, push the tip directly into the wood, taking care not to apply too much pressure as the tip may deform. If the tip cools, lift it off the wood while it regains its heat, then apply again. To cut shapes, use the side of the tip and move it in a slow sawing action to make the shape of the cut-out or bowl edge required.

Work in a well-ventilated room, as the smoke from the burning wood can get in the eyes and set off your smoke alarms.

Burning the rim with the pyrography tool

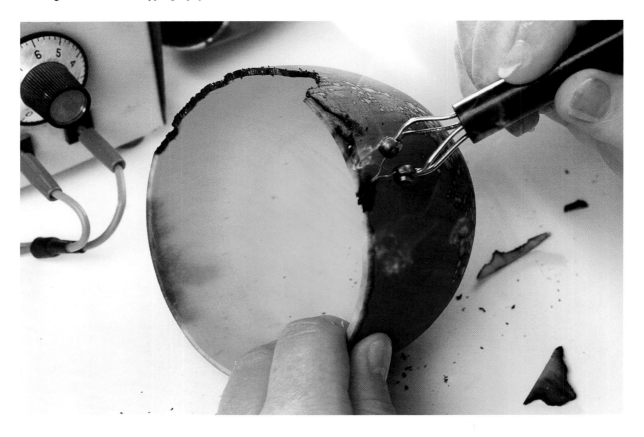

A group of Coloured series bowls in end-grain sycamore, pith not included

Materials

Water-based dyes

Domestic bleach

Water

Powder colour, Brusho or similar

Permanent coloured drawing inks

Equipment

Rubber gloves and protective apron

Pyrography machine, Peter Child or similar

Toothpicks

Cloths and tissues

Sponges

Large, soft Chinese brushes

Jam jars, one for each colour

Bowl for water

Marbling

In 1995 we were at the Arrowmont School of Arts and Crafts in Gatlingburg, Tennessee, running a woodturning course while simultaneously other classes were taking place in various crafts from photography to pottery. At the school, interaction between classes was encouraged. The cross-fertilization of ideas and skills is a brilliant idea, not just for the students but for instructors too. We were able to watch Mimi Schleicher demonstrate the traditional craft of marbling, which gave us a unique opportunity to try out this technique on the thin-walled turnings we had just been making in the woodturning workshop. The results were most intriguing, and we decided to experiment a bit more with this technique when we got home.

Marbling is very much associated with papermaking and bookbinding. The technique is surrounded by some mystique, and its methods have been closely guarded secrets. Turkey is generally considered to be the birthplace of watercolour marbling. Papers decorated in this way were often called 'Turkish'. However, it was from Holland that the British learned to appreciate marbling. Apparently, in the seventeenth century, Dutch toys were exported to England wrapped in layers of marbled papers. This was a scam set up in order to avoid paying the expensive import tax levied at that time on marbled goods. After these papers had been carefully unwrapped and pressed, they were then sold on to bookbinders.

Until accounts ledgers were superseded by the computer, it was usual for them to have marbled edges so that if a page was dishonestly removed it could easily be detected.

Equipment for marbling includes tubes of gouache, alum, ox-gall, marbling comb, sieve, plastic bowl and carrageen moss

Technique

The traditional watercolour marbling technique involves floating water-based colours on a gelatinous size made from carrageen moss, a type of seaweed. Ox-gall is first added to the colours to make them spread out and prevent them from sinking. A comb is then drawn across the surface to create the marbled patterns. The paper is laid on the surface, making sure that there is full contact, lifted off, rinsed, then pegged out to dry.

There are various ways of applying the colour; we use a pipette to drop colours onto the bath of size. The point of a knitting needle is drawn through the colours and finally a marbling comb is dragged across the surface to create those distinctive marbled patterns.

With a three-dimensional object like the natural-edged bowls we are decorating here, we hold the bowl – preferably using rubber gloves – and make a scooping movement through the size, ensuring that all the surfaces of the bowl, inside and out, are covered at some stage. Immediately after marbling we rinse it under the tap to wash off the carrageen size, then we allow the bowl to dry upside down.

The colours are floated on a bowl of carrageen moss size, then combed to make a marbling pattern. Using a scooping action, the bowl is dipped into the marbling bath

Turn the bowl, trying to ensure that all the surfaces have been coated

We tried varying this technique by first colouring the surface of the bowl with an acrylic wood stain. This should be coated in a mordant solution of alum and water and allowed to dry before dipping the bowl into the marbling bath; otherwise the marble colours just wash off, as we discovered.

Finally we spray a cellulose-based melamine coating over the marbled surface to protect it.

Marbling is a fascinating process, and there are whole books devoted to the subject, giving details of how to create many hundreds of patterns.

Lift out carefully, then rinse under the tap to remove any surplus size; leave upside down to dry off

Materials

Marbling inks

Gelatinous size (carrageen moss)

Ox-gall

Water

Alum

Equipment

Deep marbling bath

Pipette

Knitting needles

Newspaper

Rubber gloves

Marbling combs

Measuring jug

Inlaying with coloured resin

Previously we had looked at repairing splits and knot holes in bowls by filling them with resin. Initially we tried to disguise the repair by mixing in wood shavings with the resin, but it always seemed to look like a repair. On burred wood, however, where there is a more even distribution of natural holes, the technique gave excellent results: the fill looked more natural and blended in with the grain pattern.

We then tried to make a feature of the repair by mixing brightly coloured powder paint with the resin. Some of the repairs looked good, but the effect was very dependent on the shape of the split. We liked the contrast of the brightly coloured inlay against the white sycamore and holly, and so we investigated using this method of decoration in a more controlled way.

Turning grooves and then filling them with resin seemed the obvious way to go. The first grooves we turned were V-shaped. These were easy to fill, but, when it came to scraping off the hardened excess resin, some of the wood was also scraped away, so that the line became narrower in localized places and looked uneven. Making all the grooves square resolved this problem.

As the coloured lines are sharp, clean and crisp, they work well on the light-coloured woods we use, and because the coloured inlay is dramatic enough by itself we decided to keep the bowl shapes plain and uncluttered so that they would complement each other.

◀ **Making a feature of the splits: in this case we charred the edge of the split using the pyrography machine before filling the gap with a coloured resin**

A group of white sycamore vessels ready for decoration

Technique

When turning the grooves, care should be taken to make sure that these are shallow, square and clean-cut, with sharp edges. Do not sand, as this could soften the edges and the sharp definition of the colour will be lost. Also, leaving the cut surface gives a good key for the filler.

There are 'rapid-setting' and 'standard' epoxy resins. We prefer to use the rapid-setting, which means that everything has to be ready at the start. Have a small heap of powder colour ready on the mixing surface.

As it is necessary to overfill the grooves, we must remember to allow for this in estimating how much resin we might need; there is always going to be some left on the mixing board. Add in enough powder colour to give the resin a full depth of colour – at a guess, about 25% of the volume of the resin.

Quickly fill the groove with the mixture, ensuring that it is overfilled. We usually leave it to set for at least 24 hours, by which time the resin will be hard. (The resin might be *dry* in one hour, but it is still soft and usually peels off if we try to clean it up too soon.) Hand scrapers quickly clean off the excess, leaving a clean surface. A final rub with 240-grit abrasive brings up the colour.

Filling the groove around the rim with the resin and colour mixture. We do it quickly, as we use the rapid-setting resin, making sure that the groove is overfilled

Once fully hardened, the excess resin is scraped off with a hand scraper

Sanding the surface, using a sanding disc held in a Jacobs chuck in the lathe headstock. Wear a mask and run the dust-extraction system while doing this

Materials

Two-part epoxy resin

Powder colour

Equipment

Mixing stick – lollipop sticks are good

Palette knife

Hand scrapers

240-grit abrasive

Rubber gloves

Mixing surface, such as white card

Three finished vessels with coloured resin inlay to emphasize the rim

Bowl in holly, inlaid with two-part epoxy resin coloured with powder paint, diameter 6in (150mm). 1982

Imitation gold leaf

One of our early products was a silver wedding anniversary bowl with 25 one-shilling pieces set around the rim; this was very popular, and we were persuaded to try gold leaf when one of our customers requested a bowl for a golden wedding anniversary.

We experimented with the leaf, at first cutting it with scissors and covering large areas completely. Then we tried loosely tearing small pieces of gold leaf and applying them to a previously coloured surface in a slightly random fashion, leaving some areas deliberately uncovered. This method gave the gold leaf a lovely textural quality, the torn edges emphasizing this. Because the effect it creates is so sumptuous and rich, we tend to prefer using it on smaller pieces or small areas of larger pieces, combining it with painted surfaces. When applied over a yellow ochre or a rich red, the metallic finish and shine seems to be enhanced. We use it to highlight carving, and, once laid, it can also be etched into with a sharp instrument or carving tool. The leaf can be tricky to handle, as it is tissue-paper thin and very fragile. As we prefer the more distressed appearance, accidental tearing and creasing actually enhance the look we are trying to create, especially the hairline cracks which are a feature of gold leaf.

Silver wedding anniversary bowl inset with 25 one-shilling pieces. Sapele, finished with Danish oil. 1978

Technique

We use imitation gold leaf because the real thing can be expensive. Leaf is also available in silver, copper and a whole range of novelty textures. It can be laid straight onto bare wood or a painted surface as long as they are dry and clean.

Apply a size (adhesive) to the areas where you want the gold to adhere.

Lay the leaf on approximately 15 minutes after applying the size, while it is still slightly tacky but not wet. This is important, because if the size is too wet the gold will smudge and look dull instead of lustrous, and if it is too dry the gold leaf won't adhere.

We usually tear the gold leaf and then apply it with a soft brush, waiting at least 30 minutes before brushing off any loose bits, especially where the sheets overlap.

Finally we apply a shellac varnish (button polish/orange shellac) to knock back the metallic gleam and seal the surface.

Equipment for gold leaf application: ink, sponge, bonding agent, imitation gold leaf, shellac, brushes

Using a sponge to dab on the base colour of permanent ink

After brushing on a coat of bonding agent, leave for about 15 minutes to become tacky. Tear the pieces of gold leaf and apply with a soft, clean brush

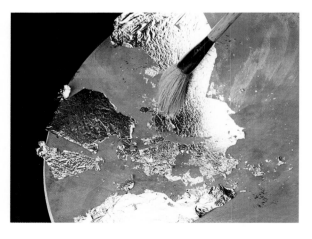

Leave to dry for at least 30 minutes, then carefully brush off any excess leaf from the unsized areas with a clean, soft brush

Seal the whole surface with a shellac varnish, applied with a soft cloth

Materials

Gold leaf

Size (adhesive)

Shellac

Equipment

Brush for applying size

Brush for applying gold leaf

Brush for removing excess gold leaf

Soft cloth for applying shellac

A selection of bowls decorated with imitation gold leaf. Here we have experimented with different base colours: yellow ochre, red and black. The rim of the small bowl was carved after the gold leaf had been applied

The rim and underside of this piece have been stained with black Indian ink

Turning sequence for end-grain bowls

1 Bowl positions in the log: two examples are shown away from the pith, one with the pith running centrally through it

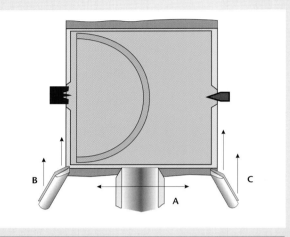

2 Blank log held between centres for initial trimming

A Clean off the bark with the spindle roughing gouge

B Square the drive end with the deep-fluted gouge

C Square off the tailstock end

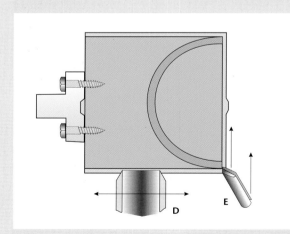

3 Blank mounted on faceplate for further truing

D A light trim to true up the blank

E Square the end

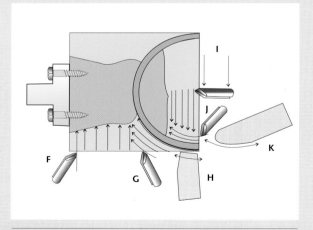

4 First stage of shaping the bowl

F Remove waste wood to make room for forming the bowl shape

G Shape the outside of the bowl

H Smooth the outside with the scraper if necessary

I Remove the bulk of the inside with gouge cuts across the surface

J Shape the inside following the outside shape

K Smooth the first section of the inside with the curved scraper

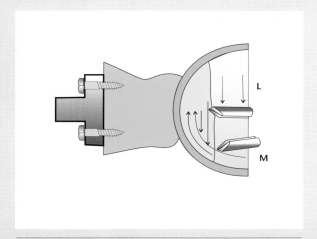

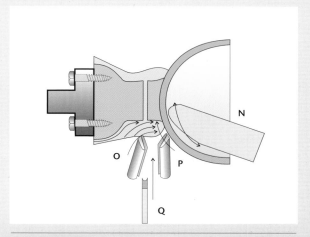

5 Completing the inside

L Make cuts across the inside of the bowl to remove the bulk of what is left

M Complete the inside shape

6 Refining the base area

N Smooth the rest of the inside with the curved scraper

O Remove waste wood to make space

P Shape around the bottom

Q Part off

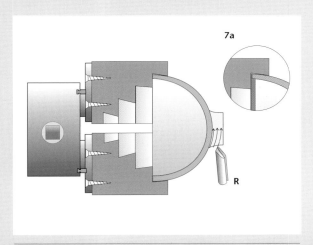

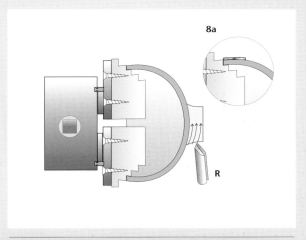

7 Finishing the underside, holding the bowl on outside of rim with wooden jaws

R Round off the bottom of the bowl

7a When the bowl is very thin, use a specially prepared disc (shaded blue) to support the rim in the chuck

8 If the rim turns inwards, hold the bowl on the inside

R Round off the bottom of the bowl

8a Add some tape to support the rim if it is very thin

Chapter 4

Pattern

Pattern, at its simplest, need be nothing more than the repetition of a line or mark. Examples of pattern can be found in architectural details such as bricks, tiling, railings and windows; these are repetitive, clearly defined, often geometric shapes and lines. Natural objects such as pebbles, plants and animals can also be a source of patterns. Often these are structures on a small scale such as leaf veins, feathers, honeycombs and seed heads.

There seems always to have been a strong instinct in people to embellish and decorate using elements of pattern. We can see evidence of this in the hand stencils discovered in prehistoric cave paintings, and the symbols and tribal images found in the early paintings of Australian Aborigines.

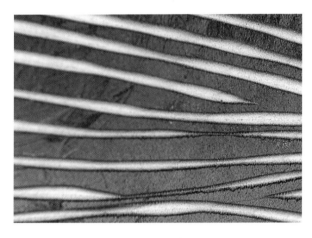

The instinct to decorate using rhythmically repeated elements must always have been strong; it is found in all human artefacts, from tribal art to the most functional of modern equipment. Similar patterns are just as prevalent in nature

Nest series

A very red earth and a big blue sky: these were our first impressions of Australia. We were there for the Wood Conference in Canberra, with a three-month workshops tour to look forward to afterwards, enabling us to see a great deal of the east coast. One of our most memorable moments was visiting an exhibition of 200 Aboriginal burial poles.

Traditionally these burial poles (so called because they are a sort of coffin for containing the bones of the deceased) are decorated with amazing patterns. Several months after death and burial, the body is exhumed and the bones are cleaned, covered in red ochre and placed inside a hollow log. These are trees, previously hollowed out by termites, which are elaborately decorated with the totemic designs of the deceased, each clan having its own recognizable symbols.

The poles in the exhibition were commissioned specially, each one representing one year of oppression by the white man. They certainly made a stunning and thought-provoking display. Individually they were impressive, but grouped together their impact was immense. It felt as if we were confronted by a motionless army standing silently in judgement, and it was made all the more relevant because this was in 1988 during the bicentennial celebrations.

Witchetty grubs, water snakes, giant goannas are the stuff of Aboriginal art. The paintings or *dreamings* tell the stories of their ancestors, their mythological creator figures, their animals, travels and adventures. The art of the Aborigines may easily be appreciated but not so easily understood.

Outsiders like ourselves are not permitted to know all the details of their sacred beliefs; however, on a superficial level we can admire their skill and dedication, and their vibrant use of colour and pattern. Liz, with her background in textile design, found the exhibitions of Aboriginal art a real inspiration with their bold use of earth colours and richly patterned surfaces.

On our return we were inspired to incorporate something of what we had seen into our own work.

Previously we had played around with a design of a round-bottomed bowl which had a wide rim below the top. We developed this idea further, widening the rim and making the bowl shallower. Our ideas were developed on a sketch pad: the wide rim would provide the painting surface, the round bottom would give some movement to the bowl. After experimenting with several prototypes, we discovered that by making the base slightly conical we could control the angle at which the bowl sat, while still retaining its life and movement.

Using acrylics, the first design for the painted rim was made up of closely interlocking quirky bird shapes incorporating lots of pattern. Our next exhibition was to be just after Easter 1988, and this prompted us to make small decorated wooden eggs; these added another dimension to the bowls, and we called them our Nest series.

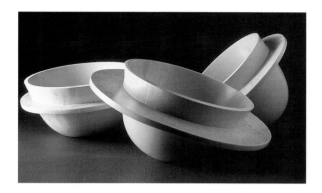

Our earlier design of wide-rimmed bowls, 1985

A display of Aboriginal burial poles, by permission of Djon Mundine (pictured at right), the curator of the 1988 exhibition. The work has subsequently been acquired by the National Gallery of Australia

Sketchbook ideas inspired by our Australian trip

A detail of the painting on a Nest series bowl

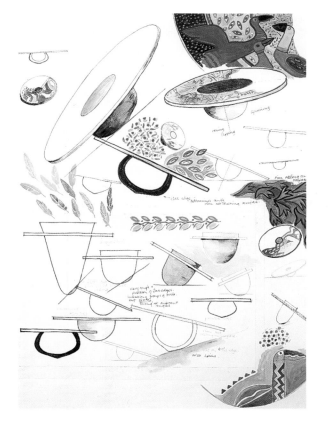

Further ideas were developed on a sketch pad. The wide rim would provide the painting surface; by making the base slightly conical we could control the angle at which the bowl sat

Quirky birds and lots of pattern painted in acrylics decorate the wide rims of these Nest bowls. Sycamore, 6–10in (150–255mm) diameter. 1988–95

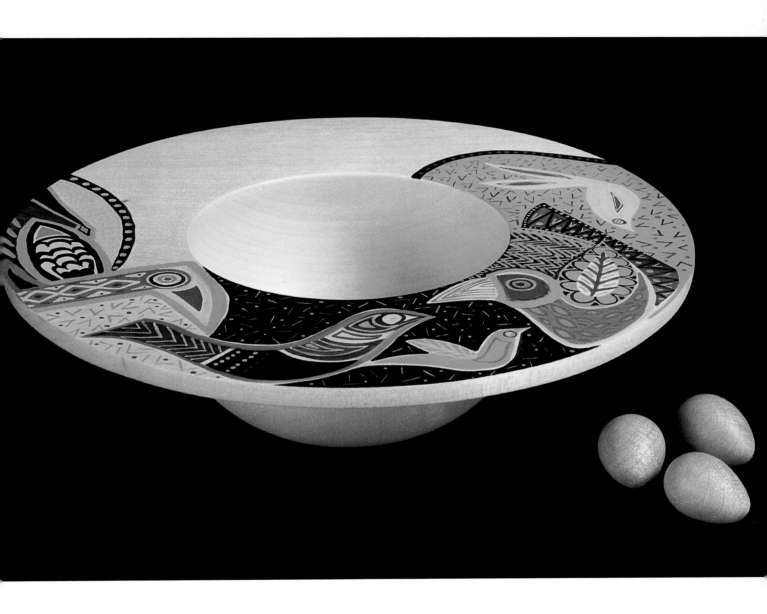

Boat series

Later, as we were playing around with the bowls, spinning them around and tipping them backwards and forwards, the movement seemed to resemble the rolling motion of a boat. We toyed with the idea of carving and painting the bowl to replicate a boat, but decided instead to draw on images from our own environment, such as harbours, boats and seagulls, in order to give a flavour of the sea.

Further inspiration came from the work of Alfred Wallis, which we first saw at the Pier Arts Centre, Kirkwall, Orkney. Born in 1855, Wallis had been a seaman before trying to scrape a living as a rag-and-bone merchant and ice-cream salesman in St Ives, Cornwall, a town which now has a large artistic community. A completely untrained artist, his work has an honest and naïve quality.

We felt that his paintings of the boats and harbours of St Ives, in muted charcoal greys, blues and yellow ochre, had a great affinity with our local fishing villages in the north of Scotland. Here the houses are often on steeply sloping roads leading down to a small slipway or harbour.

For this bowl we have painted a group of cottages, huddled together and leaning, as if sheltering from the wind and sea spray. The small boats are simplified, making an interesting repeat pattern.

It was the rocking movement of these round-bottomed bowls that first put us in mind of the motion of a boat and suggested the use of maritime images

With photographs of boats and harbours, and sketchbook drawings and paintings, we are ready to start designing the wide, painted rim of one of our Boat bowls

Liz painting a Boat bowl

Technique

The sycamore was again going to be ideal for painting on. The rim surface has to be flat, and as we are working with green wood we would need to take care in cutting the blanks from the tree. For the sake of stability, the rim had to be quarter-sawn.

The turning sequence required three chuckings: the first on a single screw to shape most of the outside, the second on a spigot at the base while the inside is turned, then the third holding on the inside of the rim while the base is finished. The procedure is illustrated on pages 118–19.

The underneath of the bowl was finished with a spray-on melamine as described on page 44. The upper rim surface and the inside were finished with a wax polish after painting with acrylics.

The wide rim provides an ideal painting surface. Images of the sea are painted in acrylics

Materials

Acrylic water-based paints

Equipment

Good-quality fine sable brushes
240-grit abrasive

The finished Boat series bowl, in sycamore, quarter-sawn at the rim, 9in (230mm) diameter. Acrylics and wax polish. 2001

Fire

We do at times describe some of our bowls as 'barbecue bowls', meaning that they are only fit for burning. It's a process that we find very therapeutic, as it clears the mind and lets you get on with the next pieces. However, when we discovered the scorched bowls by Jim Partridge at an exhibition in 1981 at the British Crafts Centre in Covent Garden, London, we realized that burning could also be a wonderful colouring and texturing process. These were such tactile pieces that we had to ignore the 'Please do not touch the exhibits' signs, picking up every one.

We tried scorching some chunky doughnut-shaped bowls and colouring the inside; however, disappointed with the results, we left them until maybe five years later when we were trying out a new carving tool. The resurrected bowls made ideal candidates for some experimental carving with our new tool. The stark contrast of a charred black surface against the smooth whiteness revealed by the carving seemed to have possibilities. We drew out some black and white patterns on paper, remembering that the cutter shapes we had lent themselves better to some designs than others.

Ideas can be drawn quickly and freely, rather like doodling, using a fairly broad, black felt-tip pen or a fine brush with white ink. Begin with simple shapes grouped together. Intricate patterns can be achieved quickly and easily if you base your patterns on the marks left by the cutting tool

Technique

Scorching can be done when the wood is either dry or green, but with very different results. A dry piece scorches very quickly and leaves a smooth, charred surface. Green wood chars slightly more slowly, but also develops surface cracking, and, if scorching is continued, some of the cracks become deep fissures which are a decorative feature in themselves.

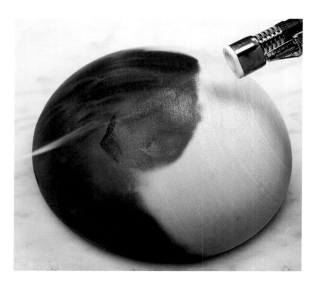

Scorching the outer surface of the bowl with a gas torch

The torch we use is small, hand-held and fuelled with butane gas (lighter fuel). It is suitable for soldering or crème brûlée. The process is very simple: the gas torch is wafted across the bowl until it is totally blackened. To finish the surface, burnish with a dry cloth (which will also remove loose black bits), preferably while the lathe is running. Apply an oil finish, such as Danish oil, and burnish dry again on the lathe. This is one of the most tactile surfaces achievable on wood.

The design is drawn with a white or light-coloured crayon pencil. We find it is best not to draw in too much detail before beginning to carve. This allows us some freedom to make small changes or adjustments as the work progresses, and if we make a slip with the carving tool there is a chance that it can still be incorporated into the final design. A loose, free design will result in a more lively piece of work as compared with a more mechanical, laboured, mathematical approach.

We use two cutter shapes: a V-shape to carve the stems and the fine lines, then a curved, gouge-shaped cutter to make the broader cuts, following the drawn lines with the power carver. Carving the wood while it is green is much easier than when it is dry.

Carving the pattern with a V-cutter in the Proxxon reciprocal carver

Materials

White crayons

Danish oil

Butane gas (lighter fuel)

Equipment

Electronic gas torch, such as Draper GT5

Reciprocating carving tool such as Proxxon MSG 220, with
    V and gouge cutters

**A selection of scorched bowls decorated with simple
carved repeat patterns**

Turning sequence for Nest and Boat series bowls

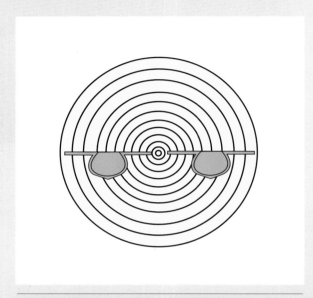

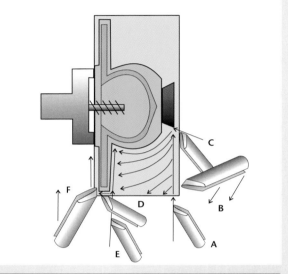

1 **Bowls in the log, avoiding the pith; the rims are quarter-cut for minimum distortion**

2 **Blank held on single-screw chuck for roughing out the outside shape**

A Square the end down to the centre

B Remove the bulk of the waste wood, following the bowl shape

C Make the spigot for the second chucking

D Trim across edge of rim

E Cut down under the rim

F Clean the top surface down to the chuck

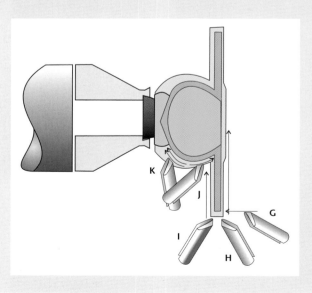

3 **Shaping the outside, with bowl held in four-jaw spigot chuck (O'Donnell jaws)**

G Trim across edge of rim

H Cut across top of rim

I Down underside of rim

J Cut the bowl shape towards the rim

K Complete the lower part with cuts towards the base

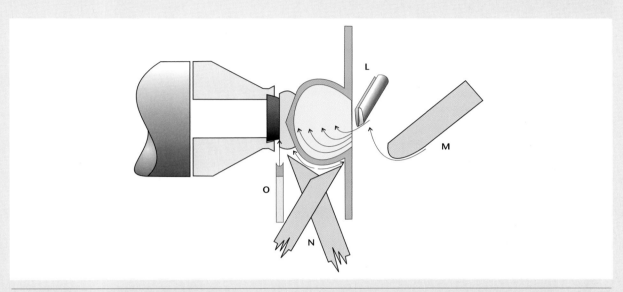

4 Completing the shape of the bowl and rim

L Hollow out the bowl

M Smooth the inside with the curved scraper

N Use skewed scrapers to refine the outside of the bowl

O Part off

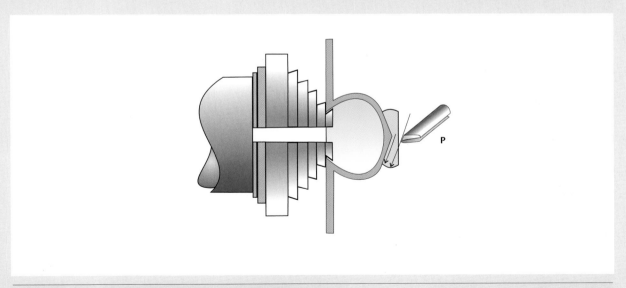

5 Holding inside the bowl with wooden jaws to finish the base

P Shape underside of bowl to the desired angle

Chapter 5

Texture

Have you noticed how young children must touch everything? In fact it seems that they don't fully know an object until they have touched it, climbed it and felt it all over. There is a very basic, almost primitive need in all of us to explore by touching, and it's true that to appreciate a form fully we need to feel as well as see. The surface texture of any form is an important element in its character: the sleekness of plastic, the roughness of concrete, the sensual feel of silk, for instance.

Wood is an amazing material which has many properties that we can explore. It is pliable, porous, combustible, durable and elastic. In creating textured surfaces we are exploiting many of these properties.

Texture may simply be the marks left by tools during production, such as the grooves left by a carving tool, or marks left by the chainsaw. Texture may be functional, creating easy-to-grip surfaces or, in a fruit bowl, allowing air to reach the underside of the fruit. Adding texture can enliven a piece by creating contrasts, drawing the eye to emphasize a shape, or catching the light to make subtle changes and shadows.

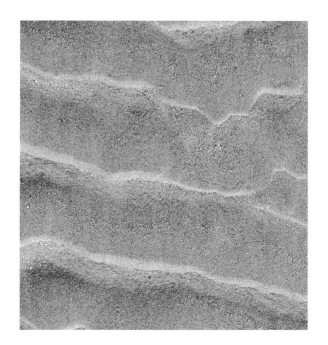

Discovering interesting textures like these prompts us to have a go at trying to achieve exciting tactile surfaces on our own work. We might experiment with carving, burning, sandblasting, rusty nails – in fact anything we can lay our hands on

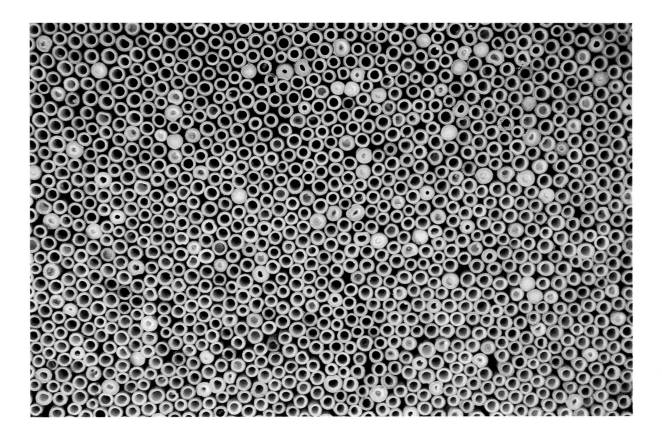

Our conical jewellery boxes were inspired by a rather improbable combination of elements: the baroque skyline of Prague, and our own collection of antique oilcans. Grouped together, with their differing heights and their decorated finials, the finished boxes evoke a fantastic medieval city

◀ A collection of our jewellery boxes with contrasting textures

A page from one of our sketchbooks exploring a variety of surface textures: knobbly pimples on the seaweed, the roughness of lichen on the rocks and the coarse hairiness of a seal pelt

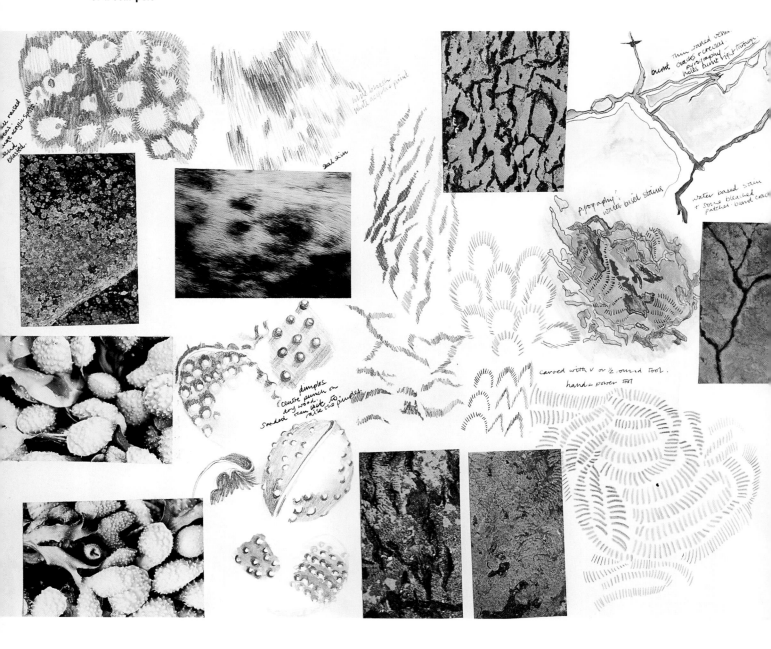

Pencil drawing of a cowrie shell, known in our part of the world as the *groatie buckie*. Looked at closely, the ridges resemble the whorls in a fingerprint ▼

Close-up studies of mushrooms, in particular the striations formed by the gills

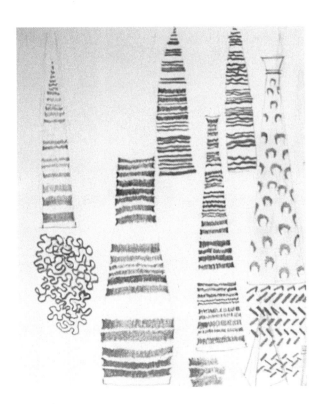

◄ Working drawings incorporating a variety of textural marks inspired by plants and lichens

Sandblasting

Our first adventure into texturing was in the mid-1980s, when we were making wooden fruit, mainly apples. The big incentive was an order to make 500 apple-shaped boxes in applewood for the *New York Times* (the Big Apple), with 'New York Times' engraved on them. Sandblasting seemed a possibility for the engraving. At the experimental stage we were fortunate to be able to use the expertise and equipment of a local glass engraver, Denis Mann (famous for engraving BBC Television's *Mastermind* trophy). While trying out sandblasting as a technique for putting letters on wood, we realized it had a greater potential for surface decoration. We explored the effect on various types of wood, both side grain and end grain, looking at pattern and texture, trying different types of masking and stencils, creating surfaces that ranged from a weathered driftwood look to finely detailed designs with crisp, hard edges.

More recently we have taken to exploring other texturing techniques – again on boxes, but this time the boxes were inspired by the unlikely combination of oilcans with brass spouts and the architectural spires and domes of Prague. The shape of the bases comes from the oilcans, while the tops reflect the embellished spires. Grouped together, they become a city of domes. The tops are turned, carved and decorated separately, then fitted to the lids. In some cases the shape of the top is reflected in the decorative patterns on the box.

The domes and towers of Prague, suitably stylized and simplified, gave rise to the finials for our turned boxes

Turning technique

The turning procedure for these conical boxes is illustrated on pages 142–3. The sequence is similar to that for other boxes with grain-matched lids. Hold between centres first to make the spigots, then separate the parts; a total of six chuckings is needed to complete the box. A well-fitting lid joint is always important for a nice box, and makes it possible to turn both parts together. As this is a very tall box, we bring up the tailstock to support the lid in the third chucking, and also to help hold the base in the jam-fitting chuck while hollowing out the underside. The final finishing is done with the tailstock removed.

Boxes with protective tape applied ready for sandblasting. Equipment needed: lane-marking tape, a cutting board from which the tape will peel off, scalpels

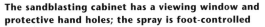

The sandblasting cabinet has a viewing window and protective hand holes; the spray is foot-controlled

Sandblasting in progress; the tape turns black when it is sprayed with grit

Sandblasting technique

Sandblasting involves an abrasive, usually aluminium oxide (not sand), propelled at the surface in a high-pressure jet of air, which then abrades the surface and eats away at the wood. This is done in a cabinet which contains the abrasive and protects the workshop atmosphere. There is a texture left by the individual abrasive grains, but also the softer part of the wood is abraded more quickly than the hard sections and therefore the grain pattern of the wood is enhanced.

To create patterns on the wood we cut shapes from a special self-adhesive tape, using a craft knife on a cutting board. We used a 'lane-marking tape'. This is a thick, slightly spongy tape which protects the wood because the abrasive bounces off it; if the tape were hard, the abrasive would eventually cut through it.

These shapes are then pressed onto the wood, creating a stencil. Because the tape is stretchy it can be manipulated around curved surfaces. The surface is now ready for sandblasting; the longer we do it, the deeper the pattern gets. When we are satisfied with the depth of cut, we remove the tape to reveal the full contrast between the smooth and the textured wood.

The complexity of the patterns can be increased by removing some pieces of tape in stages during the sandblasting, creating various levels of abrasion.

Sandblasted jewellery boxes in birch. 2001

Materials

Lane-marking tape
Aluminium oxide abrasive

Equipment

Sandblasting cabinet
Scalpels with various blades

Pimpling (*ukibori*)

Sue Wraight, a highly skilled woodcarver specializing in netsuke (Japanese carved toggles), showed us how she obtained the fascinating pimpled surface on her tiny, intricately carved netsuke in the shape of a toad. Sue created small depressions in the surface of the wood with a round-nosed hand tool, and then sanded the area down to the level of the depressions. Steaming the netsuke over boiling water caused the depressed wood to return to its original shape, creating wonderful tiny pimples, perfect for the warts on the back of a toad. The technique is known to Japanese carvers as *ukibori*.

A selection of jewellery boxes with various textures

Technique

On our larger pieces we were looking to make much bigger and bolder dimples with a stronger impact. To give us consistent additional pressure we used an engineer's automatic punch with interchangeable tips. This is spring-loaded, and fires as the nose is pressed into the wood. The interchangeable tips gave us the opportunity to make additional heads in different shapes. Using bolts with the appropriate thread, we ground and filed the head to the shape we wanted. The size of pimple we could produce was limited, as the greater the size of the tool tip, the less the wood is compressed. The wood needs to be dry; when we tried it on green wood, nothing happened.

We dimpled randomly over the whole surface of the box while it was still in the lathe, with the tailstock holding the top in position. As the dimples in our case were quite deep, we turned, rather than sanded, the excess wood away, using a large square-ended scraper, leaving the depressions just visible. After a fine sanding to finish the surface, the exciting part of the process is placing the box in a colander over a pan of boiling water to steam the wood. Putting on a lid speeds up the process, and in less than a minute the pimples have appeared like magic.

Pimpling in progress, showing the shape of the punch tip

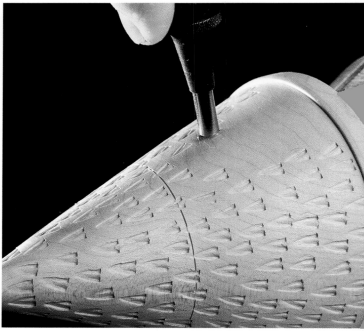

The punch is pressed into the wood until the spring fires

Steaming the box in a
colander until the
pimples appear

Materials

Boiling water

Equipment

Engineer's automatic punch with interchangeable tips

Bolts to make additional tips

Lidded pan and colander

Paper

Abrasive

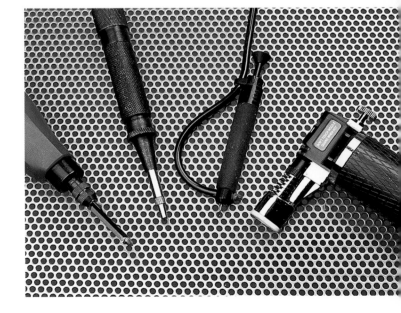

**Reciprocal carver, engineer's punch, rotary carver and gas
torch, all used in the various texturing techniques
described in this chapter**

Carving

Carving with a chisel creates crisp incised lines, which is just what we wanted to use to invoke spiral movement around the box, like tile patterns on a twisted spire.

While the box was still in the lathe with the tailstock holding the lid firmly in position, we drew a dozen evenly spaced straight lines from the base to just off centre at the top. We carved these lines with the V-tool, filling the spaces between them with shorter carved lines until the surface was full. This resulted in a very tactile, deeply ridged, slightly random surface.

Equipment

Proxxon reciprocating carver MSG 220 with V-cutter

We originally tried carving with a rotary burr when we were making the bird bowls, but the type of burrs we were using at the time quickly clogged up and the compressor had difficulty keeping up with the machine. Looking for quick, efficient ways of texturing we returned to rotary burrs, but this time with new burrs and an electric drive. The burr we used was ⅝in (8mm) in diameter; we found that using it on its side at 3000rpm removed the wood quickest, at least on sycamore. There can be a tendency for the burr to run along the surface if it is not held firmly enough against the wood, so we found that it was better to work in a pattern, making sure that untextured wood was in front of the burr so that if it did run out it didn't damage the work already done. We covered the whole box, making sure that each cut overlapped previous cuts. This resulted in a wonderful surface looking like a honeycomb.

Equipment

Proxxon rotary carver FSB 230/E with ⅝in (8mm) burr

Using the Proxxon rotary burr to create a texture all over the box

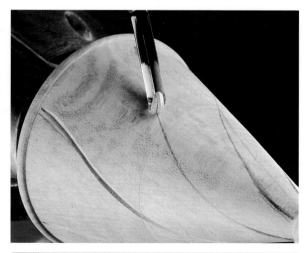

Carving a spiral groove with the Proxxon power chisel

Other effects

A wire brush is a bit like a very coarse abrasive: if it is rubbed over a rough surface on the lathe it will make the wood relatively smooth. On the other hand, if a wire brush is held stationary on a smooth piece of wood it will cut random grooves into the surface, creating a rough, distressed texture.

The brush we used was a 'spid' brush with wires 0.012in (0.3mm) in diameter. The wires are about 1in (25mm) long and bend with the wood rotation, giving a soft cutting action, so we clamped the wires together halfway down their length, which gave them a firmer cutting action and resulted in deeper cuts. With the lathe running at about 1300rpm, we held the brush firmly on the wood in a fixed position to cut the grooves, before moving to the next position along the wood.

The bead at the bottom of the box is left oversize until wire-brushing is finished, then turned down to size, leaving a smooth surface which contrasts nicely with the brushed area.

Equipment

Hand-held narrow wire brush ('spid')
Clamp or small vice to hold wires together

Wire-brushing, with a clamp attached to the wires to stiffen them

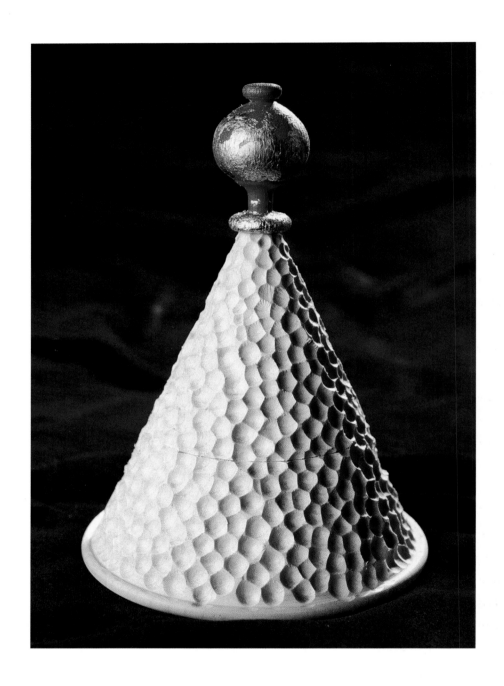

On some of the boxes we scorched over the wire-brushed surface, using the small hand-held gas torch. This had the effect of burning the rougher edges but leaving the bottoms of the grooves white. To burnish the surface we used a soft shoe brush, which removed the debris, keeping the grooves clean. A liberal amount of Danish oil was applied, as the textured surface soaks up quite a lot. It was then burnished with a cloth.

Where we wanted smooth white bands, we left these areas oversize while brushing and scorching, then turned them down to size afterwards to reveal the clean wood underneath as a nice contrast.

Equipment

Electronic gas torch such as Draper GT5

Soft brush

When it was finished, the wire-brushed and scorched box was calling out for an additional element. Some copper-headed nails we found in the workshop looked interesting, and we thought they could add a sparkle to the charred surface. We shortened the nails to ⅛in or so (4mm) so they would not protrude into the box, and drilled holes so they could be pushed in without splitting the wood, leaving the heads just proud of the surface.

Materials

Copper panel pins, ½in (13mm)

Equipment

Hammer

Pliers

Electric drill

½₂in (1mm) engineer's drill bit

Turning sequence
for conical boxes

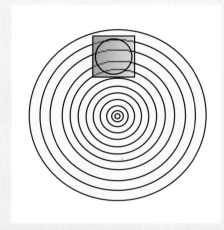

1 Where the box is located in the tree; the wood has to be kiln-dried for stability

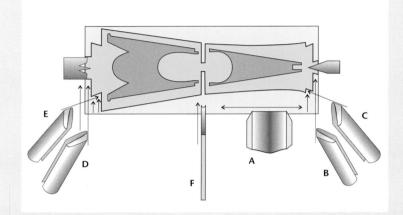

2 Blank mounted between centres for roughing out

A Round the blank with the spindle roughing gouge

B Square the tailstock end

C Make spigot on lid

D Square the drive end

E Make spigot on base

F Separate the pieces

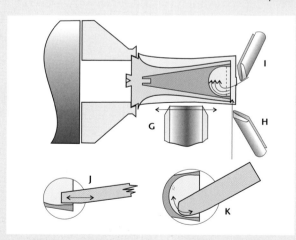

3 Lid held in spigot chuck for preliminary shaping

G Rough down the shape

H Square the joint face

I Hollow out the lid

J Use scraper to make joint surface parallel

K Smooth inside with curved scraper

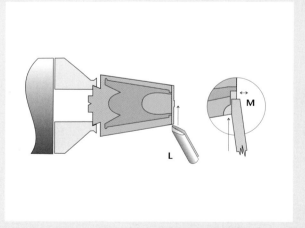

4 Base held in spigot chuck for preliminary shaping

L Square the end of the box

M Form joint surfaces with square scraper

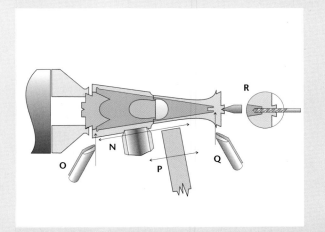

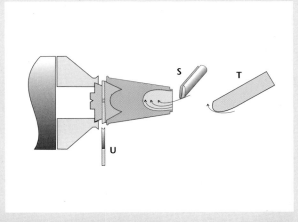

5 Lid fitted to base, with additional support from the tailstock because of the height of the box

N   Turn down outside shape

O   Square across the foot

P   Scrape/sheer-scrape to final surface

Q   Back off tailstock and square across the top

R   Drill the hole for the finial

6 Top removed to finish the base

S   Hollow the inside

T   Smooth the inside with the round-ended scraper

U   Part off the base

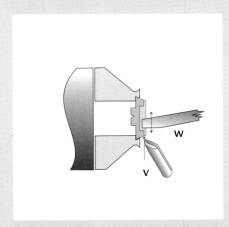

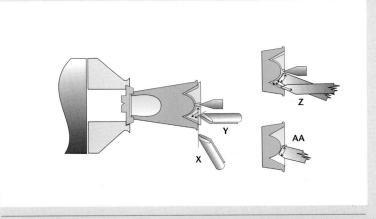

7 Making a jam-fit chuck for the base from the waste remaining in the chuck

V   Square the face

W   Form the joint faces with a square scraper

8 Finishing the underside: base held in jam chuck with light support from tailstock

X   Square the base

Y   Roughly hollow out under the base

Z   Refine the shape with scrapers

AA Finish the shape with tailstock removed

Further reading

Calvert, Ruth, and Davies, Alan, *Art and Industry since 1850* (pamphlet; Edinburgh: National Museums of Scotland, n.d.)

Harrison, Charles, and Gardiner, Margaret, *Alfred Wallis, Christopher Wood, Ben Nicholson: The Modern, the Primitive and the Picturesque* (Edinburgh: Scottish Arts Council/Pier Arts Centre, 1987)

Isaacs, Jennifer, *Australia's Living Heritage: Arts of the Dreaming* (Sydney: Lansdowne, 1984)

Pye, David, *David Pye, Woodturner and Carver* (London: Crafts Council/Bath: Crafts Study Centre, 1986)

Rowland, Kurt F., *Looking and Seeing* (4 parts; London: Ginn & Co., 1964–6)

Schleicher, Patty and Mimi, *Marbling Designs: A Complete Guide to 55 Elegant Patterns* (Asheville, NC: Lark, 1993)

Shannon, Faith, *The Art and Craft of Paper* (London: Mitchell Beazley/Il Papiro, 1987)

A useful catalogue of craft materials, including marbling equipment, imitation gold leaf, Brusho watercolour powder and shellac, is published by Specialist Crafts Ltd, PO Box 246, Leicester LE1 9QS, England.

About the authors

Liz O'Donnell trained as an artist and teacher at Liverpool College of Art, and now works as a visiting art teacher.

Michael O'Donnell is an internationally renowned turner specializing in the use of green (unseasoned) wood. His best-selling book *Turning Green Wood* is published by GMC Publications; there is also a companion video.

Liz and Michael moved to the north of Scotland in 1970, as a career move when Michael was working as a research and development engineer in the nuclear industry. Taking to the free and easy, outdoor lifestyle, they subsequently bought a croft (smallholding) on the most northerly point of the Scottish mainland.

On leaving the nuclear industry, Michael spent a period combining lighthouse keeping, landscape gardening and sea fishing, before woodturning took over as a full-time occupation, while Liz returned to teaching art.

Although Caithness is a windswept, almost treeless landscape, it became the basis for a new woodturning career, with Liz and Michael working together on decorating turned wood. This has led to them exhibiting and teaching around the world, in Scandinavia, Europe, North America, Asia and Australia. Together they have developed an attractive and innovative range of wares which combine turning with painting, staining and many other decorative techniques.

GMC Publications

BOOKS

WOODCARVING

Beginning Woodcarving	*GMC Publications*
Carving Architectural Detail in Wood: The Classical Tradition	
	Frederick Wilbur
Carving Birds & Beasts	*GMC Publications*
Carving the Human Figure: Studies in Wood and Stone	*Dick Onians*
Carving Nature: Wildlife Studies in Wood	*Frank Fox-Wilson*
Carving on Turning	*Chris Pye*
Decorative Woodcarving	*Jeremy Williams*
Elements of Woodcarving	*Chris Pye*
Essential Woodcarving Techniques	*Dick Onians*
Lettercarving in Wood: A Practical Course	*Chris Pye*
Making & Using Working Drawings for Realistic Model Animals	
	Basil F. Fordham
Power Tools for Woodcarving	*David Tippey*
Relief Carving in Wood: A Practical Introduction	*Chris Pye*
Understanding Woodcarving in the Round	*GMC Publications*
Useful Techniques for Woodcarvers	*GMC Publications*
Woodcarving: A Foundation Course	*Zoë Gertner*
Woodcarving for Beginners	*GMC Publications*
Woodcarving Tools, Materials & Equipment (New Edition in 2 vols.)	
	Chris Pye

WOODTURNING

Adventures in Woodturning	*David Springett*
Bowl Turning Techniques Masterclass	*Tony Boase*
Chris Child's Projects for Woodturners	*Chris Child*
Colouring Techniques for Woodturners	*Jan Sanders*
Contemporary Turned Wood: New Perspectives in a Rich Tradition	
	Ray Leier, Jan Peters & Kevin Wallace
The Craftsman Woodturner	*Peter Child*
Decorating Turned Wood: The Maker's Eye	*Liz & Michael O'Donnell*
Decorative Techniques for Woodturners	*Hilary Bowen*
Illustrated Woodturning Techniques	*John Hunnex*
Intermediate Woodturning Projects	*GMC Publications*
Keith Rowley's Woodturning Projects	*Keith Rowley*
Making Screw Threads in Wood	*Fred Holder*
Turned Boxes: 50 Designs	*Chris Stott*
Turning Green Wood	*Michael O'Donnell*
Turning Pens and Pencils	*Kip Christensen & Rex Burningham*
Useful Woodturning Projects	*GMC Publications*
Woodturning: Bowls, Platters, Hollow Forms, Vases, Vessels, Bottles, Flasks, Tankards, Plates	*GMC Publications*
Woodturning: A Foundation Course (New Edition)	*Keith Rowley*
Woodturning: A Fresh Approach	*Robert Chapman*
Woodturning: An Individual Approach	*Dave Regester*
Woodturning: A Source Book of Shapes	*John Hunnex*
Woodturning Jewellery	*Hilary Bowen*

Woodturning Masterclass	*Tony Boase*
Woodturning Techniques	*GMC Publications*

WOODWORKING

Advanced Scrollsaw Projects	*GMC Publications*
Beginning Picture Marquetry	*Lawrence Threadgold*
Bird Boxes and Feeders for the Garden	*Dave Mackenzie*
Celtic Carved Lovespoons: 30 Patterns	*Sharon Littley & Clive Griffin*
Celtic Woodcraft	*Glenda Bennett*
Complete Woodfinishing	*Ian Hosker*
David Charlesworth's Furniture-Making Techniques	*David Charlesworth*
David Charlesworth's Furniture-Making Techniques – Volume 2	
	David Charlesworth
The Encyclopedia of Joint Making	*Terrie Noll*
Furniture-Making Projects for the Wood Craftsman	*GMC Publications*
Furniture-Making Techniques for the Wood Craftsman	*GMC Publications*
Furniture Restoration (Practical Crafts)	*Kevin Jan Bonner*
Furniture Restoration: A Professional at Work	*John Lloyd*
Furniture Restoration and Repair for Beginners	*Kevin Jan Bonner*
Furniture Restoration Workshop	*Kevin Jan Bonner*
Green Woodwork	*Mike Abbott*
Intarsia: 30 Patterns for the Scrollsaw	*John Everett*
Kevin Ley's Furniture Projects	*Kevin Ley*
Making Chairs and Tables	*GMC Publications*
Making Chairs and Tables – Volume 2	*GMC Publications*
Making Classic English Furniture	*Paul Richardson*
Making Heirloom Boxes	*Peter Lloyd*
Making Little Boxes from Wood	*John Bennett*
Making Screw Threads in Wood	*Fred Holder*
Making Shaker Furniture	*Barry Jackson*
Making Woodwork Aids and Devices	*Robert Wearing*
Mastering the Router	*Ron Fox*
Pine Furniture Projects for the Home	*Dave Mackenzie*
Practical Scrollsaw Patterns	*John Everett*
Router Magic: Jigs, Fixtures and Tricks to Unleash your Router's Full Potential	*Bill Hylton*
Router Tips & Techniques	*Robert Wearing*
Routing: A Workshop Handbook	*Anthony Bailey*
Routing for Beginners	*Anthony Bailey*
Sharpening: The Complete Guide	*Jim Kingshott*
Sharpening Pocket Reference Book	*Jim Kingshott*
Simple Scrollsaw Projects	*GMC Publications*
Space-Saving Furniture Projects	*Dave Mackenzie*
Stickmaking: A Complete Course	*Andrew Jones & Clive George*
Stickmaking Handbook	*Andrew Jones & Clive George*
Storage Projects for the Router	*GMC Publications*
Test Reports: *The Router* and *Furniture & Cabinetmaking*	
	GMC Publications
Veneering: A Complete Course	*Ian Hosker*

GARDENING

Auriculas for Everyone: How to Grow and Show Perfect Plants
Mary Robinson
Beginners' Guide to Herb Gardening *Yvonne Cuthbertson*
Beginners' Guide to Water Gardening *Graham Clarke*
Bird Boxes and Feeders for the Garden *Dave Mackenzie*
The Birdwatcher's Garden *Hazel & Pamela Johnson*
Broad-Leaved Evergreens *Stephen G. Haw*
Companions to Clematis: Growing Clematis with Other Plants
Marigold Badcock
Creating Contrast with Dark Plants *Freya Martin*
Creating Small Habitats for Wildlife in your Garden *Josie Briggs*
Exotics are Easy *GMC Publications*
Gardening with Hebes *Chris & Valerie Wheeler*
Gardening with Wild Plants *Julian Slatcher*
Growing Cacti and Other Succulents in the Conservatory and Indoors
Shirley-Anne Bell
Growing Cacti and Other Succulents in the Garden *Shirley-Anne Bell*
Hardy Perennials: A Beginner's Guide *Eric Sawford*
Hedges: Creating Screens and Edges *Averil Bedrich*
The Living Tropical Greenhouse: Creating a Haven for Butterflies
John & Maureen Tampion
Marginal Plants *Bernard Sleeman*
Orchids are Easy: A Beginner's Guide to their Care and Cultivation
Tom Gilland
Plant Alert: A Garden Guide for Parents *Catherine Collins*

Planting Plans for Your Garden *Jenny Shukman*
Plants that Span the Seasons *Roger Wilson*
Sink and Container Gardening Using Dwarf Hardy Plants
Chris & Valerie Wheeler
The Successful Conservatory and Growing Exotic Plants *Joan Phelan*
Tropical Garden Style with Hardy Plants *Alan Hemsley*
Water Garden Projects: From Groundwork to Planting
Roger Sweetinburgh

PHOTOGRAPHY

Close-Up on Insects *Robert Thompson*
An Essential Guide to Bird Photography *Steve Young*
Field Guide to Landscape Photography *Peter Watson*
How to Photograph Pets *Nick Ridley*
LIfe in the Wild: A Photographer's Year *Andy Rouse*
Light in the Landscape: A Photographer's Year *Peter Watson*
Outdoor Photography Portfolio *GMC Publications*
Photographing Fungi in the Field *George McCarthy*
Photography for the Naturalist *Mark Lucock*
Viewpoints from *Outdoor Photography* *GMC Publications*
Where and How to Photograph Wildlife *Peter Evans*

ART TECHNIQUES

Oil Paintings from your Garden: A Guide for Beginners *Rachel Shirley*

VIDEOS

Drop-in and Pinstuffed Seats *David James*
Stuffover Upholstery *David James*
Elliptical Turning *David Springett*
Woodturning Wizardry *David Springett*
Turning Between Centres: The Basics *Dennis White*
Turning Bowls *Dennis White*
Boxes, Goblets and Screw Threads *Dennis White*
Novelties and Projects *Dennis White*
Classic Profiles *Dennis White*

Twists and Advanced Turning *Dennis White*
Sharpening the Professional Way *Jim Kingshott*
Sharpening Turning & Carving Tools *Jim Kingshott*
Bowl Turning *John Jordan*
Hollow Turning *John Jordan*
Woodturning: A Foundation Course *Keith Rowley*
Carving a Figure: The Female Form *Ray Gonzalez*
The Router: A Beginner's Guide *Alan Goodsell*
The Scroll Saw: A Beginner's Guide *John Burke*

MAGAZINES

WOODTURNING ◆ WOODCARVING ◆ FURNITURE & CABINETMAKING
THE ROUTER ◆ NEW WOODWORKING ◆ THE DOLLS' HOUSE MAGAZINE
OUTDOOR PHOTOGRAPHY ◆ BLACK & WHITE PHOTOGRAPHY
MACHINE KNITTING NEWS ◆ BUSINESSMATTERS

The above represents a full list of all titles currently published or scheduled to be published.
All are available direct from the Publishers or through bookshops, newsagents and specialist retailers.
To place an order, or to obtain a complete catalogue, contact:

**GMC Publications,
Castle Place, 166 High Street, Lewes, East Sussex BN7 1XU, United Kingdom
Tel: 01273 488005 Fax: 01273 478606
E-mail: pubs@thegmcgroup.com**

Orders by credit card are accepted

Also by Michael O'Donnell
and available from GMC Publications

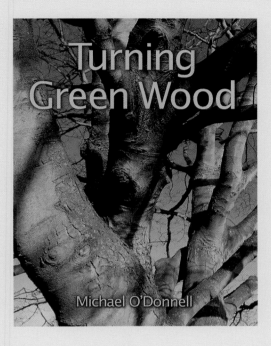

Turning Green Wood

An inspiring and thought-provoking guide to the art of turning delicate bowls and goblets from freshly felled, unseasoned wood. Using clear text and spectacular photographs to illustrate every stage, this book demystifies one of the most admired techniques used by woodturners today.

144 pages, 276 x 210mm

207 photographs

85 drawings

Full colour throughout

ISBN 1 86108 089 1

A companion video with the same title is also available. Running time 78 minutes.

ISBN 1 903521 00 9